Noel Goodey   David Bolton   Diana Goodey

Messages

Workbook

2

T0363850

My name is _____

I am in Class _____

The name of my school is _____

My English teacher is _____

My address is _____

_____

_____

Date _____

CAMBRIDGE
UNIVERSITY PRESS

1 Getting started

1 There is/There are (G) ⟶ 17a

Complete the sentences with *There's* or *There are*. Then match the sentences with the places in the box.

> Australia   London   the USA   San Francisco   New York   ~~Canada~~

1 People speak English and French here. __There are__ 7 million French speakers.   __Canada__

2 .... a big park called Central Park.   ....

3 This is a very big country in the south Pacific. .... only 20 million people.   ....

4 .... a famous bridge here, called the Golden Gate Bridge.   ....

5 .... 50 states. My favourite is California.   ....

6 .... a big clock called Big Ben.   ....

2 can/can't (G) ⟶ 11a

Complete the sentences. Use *can* or *can't* with the verbs in the box.

> walk   ~~swim~~   spell   fly   jump   speak

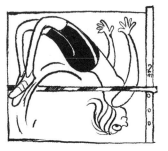

1 Martin __can't__   2 The tourist ....   3 Amy ....   4 Emma ....

__swim__ .   ... English.   .... nearly   .... on her

                                                   two metres.   hands.

5 Tom ....   6 In her dream, Kelly

....

'powerful'.

3 Word work *Odd one out*

Which word is the odd one out?

1 phone   tree   (large)   city
2 swim   sport   run   fly
3 bats   aeroplanes   tarantulas   balloons
4 eyes   spiders   wings   knees
5 cup   coffee   juice   tea
6 cheetah   owl   lion   penguin

4 *have got* 10a

Complete the sentences. Use *have/haven't got* or *has ('s) / hasn't got* with the words in the box.

> a CD player   a ticket   a cold
> a lot of homework   ~~a racket~~

2 Susan can't go to the concert because she _____ .

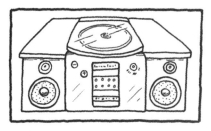

3 Jill and Ann can listen to music in bed because they _____ _____ in their room.

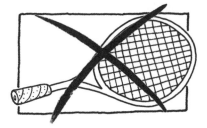

1 I can't play tennis because I *haven't got a racket* _____ .

4 Steve can't go to school because he _____ .

5 Sam and Ella can watch television this evening because they _____ _____ .

5 Reading *AfriCat*

Read the text about the AfriCat Centre. Are sentences 1–8 true or false?

Africa's 'big cats' (cheetahs, leopards and lions) are in danger. The AfriCat Centre wants to help them. The centre is in Namibia in southwest Africa. There's a hospital for the animals, and there's an education centre too.

In Namibia the big cats are a problem because they sometimes kill farm animals. The farmers often try to catch them or kill them.

A lot of tourists go to Namibia because they want to see the big cats. Tourism is important for this part of Africa. This is another reason why AfriCat wants to protect the wild animals there.

Schoolchildren from all over Namibia visit the AfriCat Centre. They meet the cheetahs, leopards and lions and they learn about the importance of helping Africa's wildlife. They try to find an answer to the question 'How can the big cats and Namibia's farmers live together?'

1 Namibia is a country in southwest Africa. *True.*

2 *In danger* means 'dangerous'. _____

3 The people at AfriCat want to save Namibia's cheetahs, leopards and lions. _____

4 The people at AfriCat want to kill farm animals. _____

5 Namibia's big cats are a problem because they kill farmers. _____

6 The big cats aren't good for tourism. _____

7 The people at AfriCat meet a lot of Namibia's schoolchildren. _____

8 'How can the big cats and Namibia's farmers live together?' This is a difficult question. _____

6 Extension *Your room*

In your notebook write a description of your room. Use *There's / There are* and *I've/We've got* or *I/We haven't got*. Write at least four sentences.

My room is quite small. There's a ...
I share the room with my brother.
We've got ....

1 Key vocabulary *Expressing opinions*

Read the sentences and then give your opinion.
Use *I agree / I don't agree* and *I think / I don't think.*

1 Matt doesn't think mobile phones are necessary.

   I don't agree. I think they're very useful.

   or *I agree. I don't think they're necessary.*

2 Ben thinks maths is boring.

   ....

   ....

3 Sadie doesn't think history is interesting.

   ....

   ....

4 Lisa thinks Manchester United is the best team in Europe.

   ....

   ....

5 Joe doesn't think computer games are very interesting.

   ....

   ....

6 Jack thinks mushrooms are delicious.

   ....

   ....

3 Listening *For and against*

🔊 Listen to Paul and Anna talking about the new sports centre in their town. Circle the right answer: a, b or c.

1 Paul doesn't think the sports centre is
   a expensive.
   ⓑ very good.
   c new.

2 Anna and Paul
   a agree.
   b have got the same opinion.
   c don't agree.

3 Paul doesn't like
   a the swimming pool.
   b basketball.
   c tennis.

4 Paul thinks the town needs
   a a skate park.
   b a skateboard.
   c a sports centre.

5 How many ball games do Paul and Anna talk about?
   a Four.
   b Five.
   c Two.

2 Vocabulary revision *Adjectives*

Complete the crossword with adjectives.

Across

5 It's very sunny. The sky's blue. It's a .... day. (9 letters)
6 The opposite of *serious*. (5)
7 This word means 'really good' and it also begins with *g*. (5)

Down

1 Everyone likes Sadie. They always say, 'Sadie's ....' (4)
2 This word means 'very bad'. (5)
3 This word describes James Bond films. (8)
4 This word means 'really fantastic'. (9)
5 The opposite of *interesting*. (6)

4 Object pronouns: *him/her/it/them* (G)→ 28a, 28b, 28c, 28d

Write sentences. Use the words in the box + *him, her, it* or *them*.

I like (x 2)   Can I speak to   ~~I can't find~~   I never wear   I don't like

1 Where are my glasses?
I can't find them.

2 You can have this T-shirt.
....

3 What do you think of my new trainers?
....

4 ....
....

This is Ms Dynamite.

5 I've got a message for Mr Grant. ....
....

6 What do you think of the pizza?
....

5 Extension *Giving your opinion*

Write your opinion about at least three things/people. You can write about the things/people in the box or you can choose others.

the food in the school canteen   the Harry Potter films   computer games
geography   Real Madrid   rap music

I don't think the Harry Potter films are very good.

....

....

....

....

....

1 Key vocabulary *Interests and activities*

What are their interests? Match the people with the words in the box.

> computer games   swimming   ~~meeting friends~~
> horror films   using the Internet   going shopping
> athletics   going out

I see Jack and Helen every Saturday. We sit in a café and talk.

What are the shops like here?

1 *meeting friends*   2 _____

It's great. They've got a new 50-metre pool at the sports centre.

I've got *Voices in the night* on video. It's really scary. I love it!

3 _____   4 _____

It's called *Megatron*. Do you want to play it?

I can run 100 metres in 12.5 seconds.

5 _____   6 _____

I hate staying at home in the evening.

I've got a website now. It's www.tomsharp.co.uk.

7 _____   8 _____

2 *like/enjoy/hate* + *-ing*   14a

Make sentences.

1 what / Ben / like / do?

   What does Ben like doing?

2 Matt / enjoy / read / astronomy magazines.

   _____

3 Sadie / not like / watch / football on TV.

   _____

4 Joe / hate / get up / on Monday morning.

   _____

5 Kate / like / live in Bristol?

   _____

3 Personal questions

Complete the questions.

1 You want to know where someone lives.

   Where do you live?

2 You want to know someone's mobile number.

   _____ your mobile number?

3 You want to know if someone can speak Italian.

   _____ you _____ Italian?

4 You want to know what sort of food someone likes.

   _____ you like?

5 You want to know if someone has got any brothers.

   _____ brothers?

6 You want to know what someone's favourite subjects are.

   _____ your favourite subjects?

4 Extension *Can I ask you some questions?*

Write at least three more personal questions.

What's your favourite sport?
Do you like swimming?

_____

_____

_____

Unit 1 Learning diary

Date _____

At the end of Unit 1, I can:

	Easy	Not bad	Difficult
give my opinion.	☐	☐	☐

I think it's _____ . I don't think it's _____ .

What do you think of _____ ? I like _____ *(it/him/her/them)*.

	Easy	Not bad	Difficult
agree and disagree.	☐	☐	☐

I agree. / I don't _____ . I agree _____ you.

	Easy	Not bad	Difficult
talk about things I like and don't like.	☐	☐	☐

I like _____ .

I don't like _____ .

	Easy	Not bad	Difficult
give details about myself.	☐	☐	☐

My address is _____ .

I've got _____ .

I can _____ .

My favourite subject at school is _____ .

	Easy	Not bad	Difficult
ask about people's interests.	☐	☐	☐

Do you like _____ ? Can you _____ ?

What's your favourite _____ ?

What sort of _____ do you like?

KEY WORDS

Adjectives

funny _____

stupid _____

_____ _____

_____ _____

Interests and activities

computer games _____

going out _____

_____ _____

_____ _____

Unit 1 was

interesting ☐   quite interesting ☐   not very interesting ☐

2 A slice of life

1 Present simple: *He lives ...* Ⓖ▸ 1a, 1c

Complete the sentences. Use the right form of the verbs in the box.

~~live~~ have got play fly go snow

1 Dan ____lives____ in Alaska.

2 It _____ a lot in Alaska.

3 Dan _____ to school on a skidoo.

4 At weekends he _____ basketball.

5 His dad _____ a small plane.

6 He _____ to Anchorage every week.

2 Present simple: negative Ⓖ▸ 1a

Complete the text about Dan and his family. Use *don't* or *doesn't* with the verbs.

Dan ¹ ____doesn't enjoy____ (enjoy) the winter in Alaska. He ² _____ (like)
the short days and the long nights. It ³ _____ (snow) every day, but it's
always very cold. The summer is different. It's never really dark, so Dan and his brother
⁴ _____ (go) to bed before twelve o'clock at night. Their parents
⁵ _____ (care) because the boys are on holiday. In the summer Dan
⁶ _____ (go) to school for three months!

3 Reading *Antarctica*

Read the text about Antarctica. Then read the sentences and write *T* (true), *F* (false) or *?* (the answer isn't in the text).

To the south of South America, there's a cold and empty continent: Antarctica. There aren't any roads or towns, but there are several research stations. About 4,000 scientists from all over the world work there for short periods. No one lives in Antarctica all the time – only millions of penguins!

The weather is always cold and windy. In June (Antarctica's winter) the temperature at the Vostock Research Station is −60°C, and it's dark all the time. In January (Antarctica's summer) the temperature is about −18°C, and it's light all the time.

Antarctica has got mountains, volcanoes and fantastic wildlife.

Every year thousands of tourists visit the continent. Some people are worried. They don't want a lot of tourists in this wild and beautiful place.

1 Antarctica is in South America.   *F*

2 There are roads between the research stations.   ....

3 Scientists study the penguins in Antarctica.   ....

4 It never rains in Antarctica, but it snows a lot.   ....

5 When it's winter in Europe, it's summer in Antarctica.   ....

6 People at the research stations don't work in June, because it's −60°C.   ....

7 It's completely dark at night in the Antarctic summer.   ....

8 The Antarctic is wild and beautiful, but tourists don't want to go there.   ....

4 Present simple: questions and short answers Ⓖ▶ 1b

Complete the questions and write the short answers.

These people work at a research station in the Antarctic. Here are the languages they speak.

	English	Spanish	French	Arabic	Italian
Marie	✔	✘	✔	✔	✘
Luís	✔	✔	✘	✘	✔
Adriana	✔	✘	✔	✘	✔
Jamal	✔	✘	✔	✔	✘

1 *Does* Luís speak English?   *Yes, he does.*

2 .... Adriana speak Spanish?   ....

3 .... Luís and Adriana speak Arabic?   ....

4 .... Jamal speak Spanish and Italian?   ....

5 .... Marie speak Arabic?   ....

6 .... they all speak English?   ....

7 What about you? .... you speak English?   ....

5 Extension *In the evening*

What do you and your friends or family do in the evening? Write at least four sentences.

Carlos and I play cards. My dad does the crossword in the newspaper.

----

1 Key grammar G → 25a

Frequency adverbs

a Put the frequency adverbs in the right order. Start with the opposite of *never*.

sometimes   ~~never~~   often   always   usually

1 _____ 2 _____ 3 _____ 4 _____ 5 *never*

b Complete the sentences with frequency adverbs.

1 I *always* wear jeans at school.

2 I _____ go out on Saturday evening.

3 Susie _____ plays computer games.

4 I _____ argue with my friends.

5 Dave _____ uses a mobile phone.

2 Frequency adverbs: word order G → 25b

Put the words in the right order and make sentences.

1 never / go / I / swimming   *I never go swimming.*

2 music / often / to / listen / I _____

3 tidy / sister / my / often / room / her / doesn't _____

4 always / she / baseball / a / does / cap / wear ? _____

5 parents / my / always / about / worry / me _____

6 hungry / my / is / brother / always _____

7 usually / breakfast / you / what / have / for / do ? _____

8 friends / pessimistic / usually / my / aren't _____

3 Listening *Megan and her mobile*

a Listen to Megan. How often does she do each activity? Put a tick (✔) in the right box.

	always	often	usually	sometimes	never
1 She sends text messages.		✔			
2 She talks to Emma before she goes to bed.					
3 She uses the computer for her homework.					
4 She writes two or three emails a day.					
5 She plays computer games.					

b Write complete sentences about Megan.

1 *She often sends text messages.*

2 _____

3 _____

4 _____

5 _____

4 Key vocabulary
Expressions of frequency 24

Complete the questions. Then write the answers.
Use the words in the box.

once		day
twice	a	week
three times		year

1 ROSIE: I see my grandparents every Sunday.

   A: _How_ often does Rosie see her grandparents?

   B: _Once a week._

2 KATE: I wash my hair on Sunday, Wednesday
   and Friday.

   A: .... often does Kate wash her hair?

   B: ....

3 SIMON: We go on holiday in February and
   in August.

   A: .... do Simon and his family

      go on holiday?

   B: ....

4 CHARLIE: I have a shower when I get up and
   before I go to bed.

   A: .... Charlie have a shower?

   B: ....

5 SARAH: I stay with my cousin every summer.

   A: ....

      stay with her cousin?

   B: ....

6 Extension *How often?*

Write sentences about a very energetic person.
Use *always, every day, three times a week,* etc.

Fabio runs to work every day. He usually goes
to the gym four times a week.

....

....

....

....

5 Word work *Sport*

Make sentences. Use the words in the box.

go	swimming	rollerblading	running	bowling
play	basketball	volleyball		

1 Tom / once a week   2 Nick / every day

Tom goes swimming
once a week.

....

3 Kirsty / not often   4 Ruth / twice a week

....

....

5 Luke and Fiona / after   6 Alex and John / on
   school   Saturday

....

....

1 Key vocabulary *Everyday routines*

When do you do these things? Write three lists.

> ~~wake up~~   have a drink   go to bed   get undressed
> get up   go to sleep   get dressed   wash
> have something to eat   get home   get ready for school

In the morning	In the evening	Morning or evening
wake up	....	....
....	....	....
....	....	....
....	....	

2 Link words: *before, after, then, after that*

Read the information and answer the questions.

Maggie

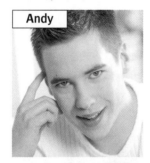
Andy

Chris

Beth

> Andy gets up half an hour before Beth gets up.
> Beth gets up ten minutes after Chris gets up.
> Maggie gets up and then Chris gets up five minutes after that.
> Maggie gets up a quarter of an hour after Andy gets up.
> Andy gets up at seven o'clock.

1 Who gets up first?   ....

2 What time does he/she get up?   ....

3 Who gets up next?   ....

4 What time does Chris get up?   ....

5 Who gets up last?   ....

6 What time does he/she get up?   ....

3 Silly sentences?

For each sentence write *OK* or *Silly*.

1 I wake up before my alarm clock rings.

   OK.

2 I have a shower after I get dressed.

   ....

3 I get undressed and then I go to school.

   ....

4 I have a bath and after that I go to bed.

   ....

5 I have a drink after I get home.

   ....

6 I get up and then I go to sleep.

   ....

4 Extension *An average day*

Imagine an average day in the life of a dog. Write at least four sentences.

Blackie usually sleeps under the table in the kitchen. He wakes up at ... and then he ...

....

....

....

....

....

....

....

....

....

....

Unit 2 Learning diary

At the end of Unit 2, I can:

	Easy	Not bad	Difficult

- talk about my daily life. ☐ ☐ ☐

  I live in _____ . *I* _____ .

- describe what other people do. ☐ ☐ ☐

  Nick lives _____ . *He* _____ .

- spell the third person form of these verbs. ☐ ☐ ☐

I play	*he plays* _____	I try	_____
I study	*he studies* _____	I wash	_____
I go	*he* _____	I have	_____
I watch	_____		

- talk about how often I do things. ☐ ☐ ☐

  I sometimes _____ . *I never* _____ .

  I _____ *a week.*

- ask about other people's daily life. ☐ ☐ ☐

  Does she _____ *to school by train?*

  _____ *your brother play* _____ *?*

  Where _____ *live?*

KEY WORDS

Frequency adverbs	**Expressions of frequency**	**Everyday routines**
always _____	*every day* _____	*get up* _____ _____
_____	*once a week* _____	_____ _____
_____	_____	_____ _____
_____	_____	_____ _____

Unit 2 was

interesting ☐   quite interesting ☐   not very interesting ☐

3 Stories

1 Key vocabulary *Numbers*

Write the answers in words.

1 thirty + thirteen = *forty-three*

2 twelve + eleven = _____

3 five point six + one point seven =

_____

4 eight point four − one point three = _____

5 two hundred and seven + nine hundred and thirteen =

_____

6 three million, one hundred thousand − two hundred and ten thousand =

_____

2 Key vocabulary *Months*

Find the 12 months and answer the questions.

E	S	J	A	N	U	A	R	Y
N	E	B	N	M	A	U	O	F
O	P	T	O	A	P	G	C	E
J	T	U	V	L	R	U	T	B
U	E	M	E	C	I	S	O	R
L	M	A	M	E	L	T	B	U
Y	B	R	B	M	A	Y	E	A
D	E	C	E	M	B	E	R	R
I	R	H	R	J	U	N	E	Y

1 Which month begins with the fourth letter of the alphabet? *December*

2 Which two months begin with the first letter? _____ _____

3 Which month begins with the sixth letter? _____

4 Which three months begin with the tenth letter? _____

_____ _____

5 The third and the fifth months of the year begin with the same letter. What are

they? _____ _____

6 What are the other three months? _____ _____

_____

3 Key vocabulary *Dates*

Write these dates in words.

1 1/9/2006   *the first of September, two thousand and six*

2 3/3/1999   _____

3 5/11/2010   _____

4 8/7/2004   _____

5 31/12/1986 _____

6 22/2/1990   _____

7 4/6/2000   _____

8 6/8/1995   _____

4 Past simple: *was, were* 4a

Complete the text with *was* or *were*.

Marilyn Monroe ¹ _____was_____ an American film star. She ² _____ born in 1926. Her real name ³ _____ Norma Jean Baker. Her most famous films ⁴ _____ *Gentlemen Prefer Blondes* (1953) and *Some Like it Hot* (1959). The baseball player Joe DiMaggio and the writer Arthur Miller ⁵ _____ two of Marilyn's husbands. She ⁶ _____ a very popular actress and, when she died in 1962, people all over the world ⁷ _____ very sad.

5 Past simple: regular verbs 2a

Last weekend was special for these young people. Complete the sentences. Use the past simple form of the verbs.

| travel walk sail play finish ~~use~~ |

1 Dylan ___used___ his new skateboard for the first time.

2 Molly _____ across the lake on her own.

3 Pete _____ to London on his own.

4 Lee _____ thirty kilometres.

5 Julie _____ her Harry Potter book.

6 Jamie _____ for his school team for the first time.

6 Extension *An exciting weekend*

Imagine that last weekend was a special time for you. What did you do? Write one or two sentences. Choose from these verbs: *talk, play, travel, use, visit, watch.*

Last weekend I talked to ...

....

....

1 Key vocabulary *Holidays*

Match the words in A with the words in B and make sentences.

A	B
1 We had a holiday	a in the sea.
2 We travelled	b only had two beds.
3 My friend travelled by	c the beach.
4 I carried all my things	d in a tent.
5 We stayed at	e in Portugal last summer.
6 We never	f a campsite.
7 My parents' caravan	g my new sleeping bag.
8 My friend and I slept	h by ferry.
9 I was very comfortable in	i in a rucksack.
10 Every day we went swimming	j stay at a hotel.
11 We often played volleyball on	k plane from London.

1 *e*   2 ____   3 ____   4 ____   5 ____   6 ____   7 ____   8 ____   9 ____   10 ____   11 ____

2 Past simple: irregular verbs 3a

a Complete the crossword with the past simple form of the verbs.

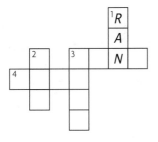

Across	Down
3 go	1 run
4 come	2 see
5 sleep	3 be
8 take	5 say
9 have	6 put
	7 get

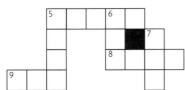

b Complete the sentences with verbs from 2a.

1 Hannah usually sleeps for eight hours every night, but last night she _____*slept*_____ for twelve hours.

2 Joe and Sadie usually have cereal for breakfast, but yesterday they _____ toast.

3 Lisa usually gets about three emails a day, but yesterday she _____ ten!

4 Sally usually goes rollerblading at the weekend, but last weekend she _____ swimming.

5 Mrs Taylor usually takes her children to the park on Saturday, but last Saturday she _____ them to the cinema.

6 Gemma doesn't usually see her boyfriend during the week, but last week she _____ him on Monday and Wednesday.

7 Matt usually puts ham in his sandwiches, but yesterday he _____ cheese in them.

8 Lee doesn't usually run to school, but he _____ this morning because he was late.

3 Reading *Alone across the Atlantic*  3a

Complete the text about Seb Clover. Use the past simple form of the verbs.

In 2003 an English boy, Seb Clover, [1] _sailed_ (*sail*) across the Atlantic on his own. He [2] _____ (*go*) from Tenerife to Antigua in 25 days. He [3] _____ (*be*) only 15 years old.

The 25 days [4] _____ (*be*) often difficult. One day, in the middle of the Atlantic, he [5] _____ (*see*) some whales. He was a bit scared when they [6] _____ (*come*) just two metres from the boat.

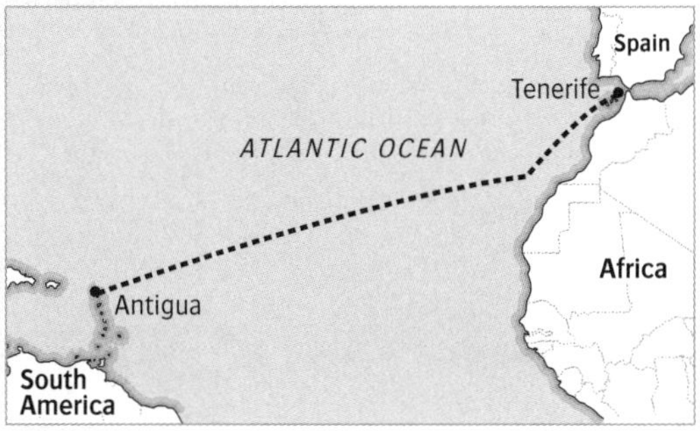

Another problem was food. Three days before he [7] _____ (*arrive*) in Antigua, he [8] _____ (*eat*) his last piece of chocolate!

In Antigua he was a hero. He [9] _____ (*have*) a great time. In the streets, everyone [10] _____ (*want*) to say hello to him. He was on TV and in newspapers all over the world. But a week later he [11] _____ (*get*) a plane to England and then he [12] _____ (*go*) back to school.

Map labels: Spain, Tenerife, ATLANTIC OCEAN, Africa, Antigua, South America

4 Listening *Adam's weekend*

Listen to Adam talking about his weekend. Circle the right answer: a, b or c.

1 On Saturday Adam and Pete
   a went to a campsite.
   b slept on the beach.
   c played football.

2 In the afternoon they
   a played volleyball.
   b went swimming.
   c had lunch at the café.

3 They went to bed at
   a about 10 o'clock.
   b about 10.30.
   c 1 o'clock.

4 In the night
   a they slept for eleven hours.
   b someone came into the tent.
   c it rained.

5 They had a problem.
   a Their sleeping bags were too short.
   b Someone was in their tent.
   c Their tent had a hole in it.

6 On Sunday morning
   a they went home.
   b it started to rain.
   c they went on a boat trip.

5 Extension *Find the verbs*

Find ten irregular past simple verbs in the wordsnake. Write them with their infinitive form.

abccamedetookagotowenteputsaiduhadisawsleptoran

1	_came_	_come_	6	_____	_____
2	_____	_____	7	_____	_____
3	_____	_____	8	_____	_____
4	_____	_____	9	_____	_____
5	_____	_____	10	_____	_____

If you like, make another wordsnake and ask a friend to find the words.

1 was, wasn't, were, weren't ⒢ 4a

Underline the right verb form.

1 I had a good holiday, but the weather (*was* / <u>*wasn't*</u>) very good.
2 I (*was* / *wasn't*) ill at the weekend, so I stayed in bed.
3 My parents (*were* / *weren't*) very happy because I came home late.
4 The exam was awful. The questions (*were* / *weren't*) really difficult.
5 I wanted to buy a new skateboard, but the shop (*was* / *wasn't*) open.
6 The CDs (*were* / *weren't*) expensive, so I bought three.

2 Past simple: negative ⒢ 2a, 3b

Write a negative sentence and an affirmative sentence for each picture. Use the verbs in the box.

| go   invent   come from   go across |

   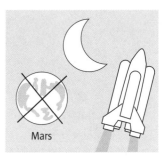

1 Marconi *didn't invent the mobile phone.*

He ....

....

2 Seb Clover ....

....

He ....

....

3 The Beatles ....

....

They ....

....

4 Apollo 11 ....

....

It ....

to the moon.

3 Word work   *The ballad of Billy Magee*

Write the words.

1 A sort of policeman in the USA.   s <u>h</u> <u>e</u> <u>r</u> <u>i</u> <u>f</u> <u>f</u>
2 The opposite of *easy*.   h __ __ __
3 Bill works with Fiona, and Fiona works with Bill. They work ....   t __ __ __ __ __ __ __
4 Bill loves Fiona and Fiona loves Bill. They're ....   i __ __ __ __ __ __
5 Nick hasn't got any grandparents now. They're all ....   d __ __ __
6 This verb means 'to take something that doesn't belong to you'.   s __ __ __ __
7 We say: 'I don't ......' when something doesn't worry us.   c __ __ __

4 Extension   *They were different*

When your parents were teenagers, they probably weren't the same as you and your friends.
Think of at least three differences and write sentences. Use *didn't* + *listen to, wear, go, have*, etc.

They didn't listen to hip-hop. They didn't wear ...

....

....

....

Unit 3 Learning diary

Date _____

At the end of Unit 3, I can:

	Easy	Not bad	Difficult
say dates.	☐	☐	☐

My birthday is on _____ .

use the past simple form of regular and irregular verbs.   ☐ ☐ ☐

Present	Past	Present	Past	Present	Past
arrive	arrived	live		sleep	
be	was/were	play		stay	
come	came	put		take	
get		run		travel	
go		say		use	
have		see		walk	

	Easy	Not bad	Difficult
talk about events in the past.	☐	☐	☐

I was born _____ .

Yesterday I _____ .

	Easy	Not bad	Difficult
use the past simple negative.	☐	☐	☐

I wasn't _____ when I was little.

We didn't _____ at school yesterday.

Billy Magee _____ .

KEY WORDS

Numbers

3	three	7	
13	thirteen	17	
30	thirty	70	
13th	thirteenth	17th	
30th	thirtieth	70th	

Holidays

caravan _____   _____

_____

_____

_____

Unit 3 was

interesting ☐   quite interesting ☐   not very interesting ☐

4 Entertainment

1 Word work *Verbs in the quiz*

Complete the sentences with the verbs in the box. Then write the infinitive form.

| found | bit | ~~wrote~~ | invented | took place | sold |

1 Shakespeare ___wrote___ at least thirty-seven plays. (___write___)

2 Alexander Bell _____ the telephone. (_____)

3 In 1626 the Native Americans _____ Manhattan to Holland for $25. (_____)

4 The first Olympic Games _____ in Athens in 1896. (_____)

5 A snake _____ the Egyptian queen Cleopatra and killed her. (_____)

6 Four teenagers _____ some very old paintings in a cave in France in 1940. (_____)

2 Question words

Complete the conversation with Ivan Whitfield. Use *What, Where, When, Why, How* or *Which*.

A: ¹ ___How___ old were you when you started writing?
B: I was eight.

A: ² _____ did you live when you were small?
B: In Bristol.

A: ³ _____ Bristol football team did you support, Bristol City or Bristol Rovers?
B: Bristol City, of course!

A: ⁴ _____ did you move to London?
B: In 2001.

A: ⁵ _____ was the name of your first book?
B: *A Cat Called Tiger.*

A: ⁶ _____ did you call the cat 'Tiger'?
B: Because my cat's name was Tiger.

Ivan Whitfield: writer of children's books

3 *was/were*: questions G▶ 4b

Read the information in the box and complete the questions. Use question words and *was* or *were*.

> ARSENAL played Liverpool on Saturday afternoon in Liverpool. Liverpool won, 3–2. Alan Lang got all Liverpool's goals. A lot of people didn't get tickets for the match, but they watched it on TV on Saturday night.

1 A: ___Where___ ___was___ the match?
  B: In Liverpool.

2 A: ___Who___ _____ the two teams?
  B: Arsenal and Liverpool.

3 A: _____ the match?
  B: On Saturday afternoon.

4 A: _____ the winners?
  B: Liverpool.

5 A: _____ the score?
  B: 3–2 to Liverpool.

6 A: _____ Liverpool's star?
  B: Alan Lang.

7 A: _____ the match on TV?
  B: On Saturday night.

4 Past simple: questions (G) 2b

Put the words in the right order and make questions. Then write true answers.

1 get up / this / when / you / morning / did ?
   A: *When did you get up this morning?*
   B: *I got up at*

2 breakfast / what / have / you / did / for ?
   A: _____
   B: _____

3 time / leave / did / what / you / home ?
   A: _____
   B: _____

4 like / what / weather / the / was ?
   A: _____
   B: _____

5 your / what / lesson / did / first / start / time ?
   A: _____
   B: _____

5 Past simple: more questions (G) 2b

Complete the questions.

1 A: What *did you do on Saturday* ?
   B: I went shopping.

2 A: Who _____ ?
   B: I saw Jess and Molly.

3 A: What _____ ?
   B: I bought some trousers and a new top.

4 A: Where _____ ?
   B: We had lunch in a café.

5 A: What time _____ ?
   B: We got home at about four o'clock.

6 Dialogue completion (G) 2b, 4b

What were Anna's questions? Choose the right questions from the list (a–i).

ANNA: ¹ d
MATT: It was fantastic.
ANNA: ² _____ ?
MATT: I went with my brother.
ANNA: ³ _____ ?
MATT: I bought them on the Internet.
ANNA: ⁴ _____ ?
MATT: All the songs on their new CD.
ANNA: ⁵ _____ ?
MATT: *Come into my world.*
ANNA: ⁶ _____ ?
MATT: About eleven.

a How did you get there?
b Where did you buy the tickets?
c What time did the concert finish?
d What was the concert like?
e Which song did they sing at the end?
f Were they expensive?
g Who did you go with?
h What did you do?
i Which songs did they sing?

7 Extension *Write a song!*

Imagine you're a songwriter. Write some questions in the past simple for a new pop song.

Why did you leave me? What did I say?

_____

_____

1 *was/were*: questions and short answers 4b

Put the words in the right order and make questions. Then write the short answers.

1 Elvis Presley / English / was ?

A: *Was Elvis Presley English?*

B: *No, he wasn't.*

2 George Washington / first / the / president / American / was ?

A: ....

B: ....

3 painters / were / and / Van Gogh / Cézanne ?

A: ....

B: ....

4 Sophia Loren / actress / an / was ?

A: ....

B: ....

5 were / pop group / Pilgrim Fathers / a / the ?

A: ....

B: ....

6 animal / a / real / was / Tyrannosaurus Rex ?

A: ....

B: ....

2 Past simple: questions and short answers 2b, 3b

Write a question and a short answer for each picture. Use the verbs in the box.

beat   catch   bite   phone   ~~enjoy~~   win

1 you/it?

A: *Did you enjoy it?*

B: *No, I didn't.*

2 you?

A: ....

B: ....

3 it/you?

A: ....

B: ....

4 he/the American champion?

A: ....

....

B: ....

5 you/anything?

A: ....

....

B: ....

6 David/you?

A: ....

....

B: ....

3 Reading J.R.R. Tolkien (G) ➔ 2b, 4b

Read the text about Tolkien. Then complete the questions and write short answers.

John Ronald Reuel Tolkien was English, but he was born in South Africa in 1892. Both his parents died when he was a boy, so John went to live with an aunt in England. After he left school, he went to Oxford University and studied English. Then he got a job as a teacher at the university.

Tolkien had four children and he often told them stories. They really enjoyed one story. It started: 'In a hole in the ground lived a hobbit …' This story became Tolkien's first book, *The Hobbit*. He later wrote *The Lord of the Rings*. Both books were fantastically popular, especially in the USA. Tolkien became rich and famous, but he hated being well known.

Tolkien created an imaginary world called 'Middle Earth' for his stories. He invented special languages for Middle Earth, and he could speak and write these languages!

He died in 1973. Thirty years later, the New Zealand film director Peter Jackson made three films of *The Lord of the Rings*. They were big hits all over the world.

1 A: *Was*_____ Tolkien born in England?

  B: *No,*_____

2 A: _____ his father die when Tolkien was young?

  B: _____

3 A: _____ he go to live with his grandmother?

  B: _____

4 A: _____ his children like the story about the hobbit?

  B: _____

5 A: _____ *The Lord of the Rings* his first book?

  B: _____

6 A: _____ his books popular in the USA?

  B: _____

7 A: _____ Middle Earth a real world?

  B: _____

8 A: _____ Tolkien work with Peter Jackson?

  B: _____

4 Listening / Key vocabulary Jobs

Who are the eight people talking to? Use the words in the box.

| builder | disc jockey | mechanic | ~~waitress~~ | shop assistant | farmer | secretary | taxi driver |

1 *waitress*_____   4 _____   7 _____

2 _____   5 _____   8 _____

3 _____   6 _____

5 Extension What did you do yesterday?

Choose one of the jobs in Exercise 4. Imagine you're that person. Write about what you did yesterday.

I'm a disc jockey. I started work at …

_____

_____

1 Key vocabulary *Past time expressions*

Write the missing time expressions.

1 in 2002	*in 2003*	in 2004
2 in July	....	in September
3 on Tuesday	....	on Thursday
4 last week	two weeks	three weeks ago
5 this year	last year	two years ....
6 .... month	last month	two months ago
7 yesterday morning	yesterday	yesterday evening
8 yesterday afternoon	yesterday evening	last ....

2 Time expressions with *ago*

Make complete sentences with *the first ...* and *... years ago*. Then match the sentences with the pictures.

1 George Beauchamp / make / first electric guitar (1928)

George Beauchamp made the first electric guitar ... years ago.   Picture **C**

2 Clarence Saunders / open / first supermarket (1916)

....

....   Picture ......

3 Igor Sikorsky / invent / first helicopter (1939)

....

....   Picture ......

4 Yuri Gagarin / become / first spaceman (1961)

....

....   Picture ......

5 James A. Naismith / play / first game of basketball (1891)

....

....   Picture ......

A

B

C

D

E

3 Extension *When did it happen?*

Write about at least three important events in the past. Use verbs in the past simple and *ago*.

Lazio won the Championship ... years ago. I was born ... ago.

....

....

....

Unit 4 Learning diary

Date ....

At the end of Unit 4, I can:

	Easy	Not bad	Difficult
use question words.	☐	☐	☐

Where? = ... (in my language)

Who? = ... When? = ... What? = ... Why? = ...

Which? = ... How? = ...

	Easy	Not bad	Difficult
ask and answer questions about things and people in the past.	☐	☐	☐

.... were the Beatles?

.... did Clare Burgess do at university?

.... Tolkien a film director?   No, he ....

.... Clare like her first job?   Yes, she ....

.... John Lennon live in Hollywood?   No, he ....

	Easy	Not bad	Difficult
say when things happened in the past.	☐	☐	☐

Yesterday afternoon I ....

Last night I ....

I went to the cinema .... ago.

three weeks ago = ... (in my language)

	Easy	Not bad	Difficult
describe different jobs.	☐	☐	☐

My uncle's a taxi driver.   My ....

I want to be ....

In English we use .... or *an* with the names of jobs.

KEY WORDS

Jobs

builder ....

....

....

....

Past time expressions

last night ....

....

....

....

Unit 4 was

interesting ☐   quite interesting ☐   not very interesting ☐

5 On the move

1 Key vocabulary *In town*

Match the things/people with the places. Write the letters A–J.

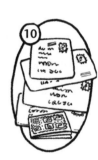

A	hospital
B	bank
~~C~~	~~car park~~
D	department store
E	post office
F	police station
G	clothes shop
H	newsagent's
I	shoe shop
J	chemist's

1 C   2 _____   3 _____   4 _____   5 _____   6 _____   7 _____   8 _____   9 _____   10 _____

2 Key vocabulary *Directions*

Give directions to the Internet café. Complete the sentences with the words in the box.

Go across   Go along   Go past   turn left   Turn right   ~~at the end of~~   on the left   on the right

1 There's a big square *at the end of* this street.

2 _____ the square.

3 _____ and you're in Mill Street.

4 _____ Mill Street.

5 _____ the hospital.

6 Then _____ and you're in Park Road.

7 There's a car park _____ and the Internet café is _____ .

3 Word work *Prepositions of place*

Describe where Lightning is in each picture. Use the prepositions in the box.

| opposite | next to | outside | ~~behind~~ | in |

1 Behind the tree.

2 _____

3 _____

4 _____

5 _____

4 Listening *Can you tell me the way?*

James is outside the station. Listen to two people giving him directions to the football stadium. Who's right? Put a tick (✓) in the right box.

The man ☐   The woman ☐

```
                              park              football
   school                                       stadium

              London Road

   Queen's                            
   Hotel          supermarket          car park

              Silver Street
   post                                department
   office    chemist      newsagent    store

   bank                                police station
                 South Street
   James
   station   town    library  hospital
             hall
```

Station Road · Oak Street

5 Extension *The way to my house*

Imagine that your English teacher is coming to your house in his/her car. He/She doesn't know the way. Write directions.

Turn right at the school gate. Go along … Go past … I live at number …, on the … floor.

_____
_____
_____
_____
_____
_____
_____

1 Present continuous: affirmative 5a

Complete the two poems. Use the present continuous form of the verbs in the boxes. Then answer questions a–d.

Poem 1

wait   look   ~~sit~~   eat

We ¹ *'re sitting* on the platform.

We ² .... for our train.

My friend ³ .... peanuts.

I ⁴ .... at the rain.

Poem 2

stand   have   shout   swim

Dave ⁵ .... a scary dream.

He ⁶ .... in the dark.

His friends ⁷ .... on the beach.

They ⁸ ....: 'Dave! A shark!'

a   Where are they?

They're at ....

b   What's the weather like?

It ....

c   Where is Dave, in his dream?

He's in ....

d   Why is he scared?

A shark .... (*come*)

2 Present continuous: negative 5a

Complete the sentences. Use the negative form of the present continuous.

1   Can I come to town with you? I *'m not doing* (*do*) anything at the moment.

2   You can have our tennis rackets. We .... (*use*) them at the moment.

3   We can go for a walk. It .... (*rain*) now.

4   I'm trying to phone Nick, but he .... (*answer*).

5   Kate's at the cinema, but she .... (*watch*) the film. She's asleep!

6   Tom and Dave .... (*listen*) to the teacher. They're bored.

3 Present continuous: questions 5b

a   Put the words in the right order and make questions.

1   you / what / doing / are ?
What are you doing?

2   his / your / dad / job / new / is / enjoying ?
....

3   going / you / where / are ?
....

4   Kate / are / to / and / Helen / bed / going ?
....

5   why / you / are / shouting ?
....

b   Match the questions in 3a with the answers.

a   No, it's really boring.
b   To the sports centre
c   ~~I'm looking for my mobile.~~
d   Because I'm angry
e   Yes, they're very tired.

1 _c_   2 ......   3 ......   4 ......   5 ......

4 Dialogue completion

Complete the conversation. Choose the right sentences from the list (a–g).

BETH: Look, Anna. Is that Dave over there at the bus stop?

ANNA: Yes, it is. ¹ _f_

BETH: I think it's Janet Smith.

ANNA: Janet Smith? ² ....

BETH: I'm not sure, but they're having a great conversation!

ANNA: ³ ....

BETH: Yes, I can see. Perhaps they're going to the football match.

ANNA: ⁴ ....

BETH: I know.

ANNA: ⁵ ....

BETH: Well, I know Janet's crazy about football. And perhaps Dave's crazy about Janet!

a But Dave doesn't like football.

b Why's he talking to her?

c What's her name?

d Why's he going to the match, then?

e Dave and Janet are going to the match.

f ~~Who's he talking to?~~

g They're wearing blue and white scarves.

5 Reading   *Real or a copy?*

Look at the three paintings. One of them is the real painting by Pietro Doli. The other two are copies. Read the description of the real painting and decide if it is A, B or C.

.... is the real Pietro Doli painting.

The Gift by Pietro Doli

In Doli's painting *The Gift* a woman is standing under an apple tree. She's tall with long fair hair. She's wearing a long white dress and a necklace with a silver star. She's smiling. In her right hand, she's holding an apple, and there are several apples on a table next to her. There's also a cage on the table. The cage door is open and a bird is flying out. At the woman's feet, two little children are playing with a ball. The ball is our planet, the Earth.

6 Extension

What's happening?

Find an interesting picture or photo and write about it in your notebook. Describe the place. What are the people in the picture doing?

1 Present continuous or present simple? 5c, 1c

Choose two true sentences for each picture.

1 (a) Susie drinks coffee.
   b Susie doesn't drink coffee
   c Susie is drinking coffee.
   (d) Susie isn't drinking coffee.

2 a Liam doesn't play the guitar.
   b Liam is playing the guitar.
   c Liam plays the guitar.
   d Liam isn't playing the guitar.

3 a John isn't working at the moment.
   b John works.
   c John is working at the moment.
   d John doesn't work.

4 a Jenny is wearing her glasses.
   b Jenny wears glasses.
   c Jenny isn't wearing her glasses.
   d Jenny doesn't wear glasses.

2 What am I doing? 5c, 1c

Complete the text. Use the present simple or the present continuous form of the verbs.

This is Fran Baker. She ¹ ___comes___ (come) from England. She ² _____

(work) as a waitress in London. She isn't usually a very adventurous person.

She ³ _____ (not like) dangerous sports and she ⁴ _____ (hate)

heights! At the moment Fran's on holiday in New Zealand. She ⁵ _____ (do)

a bungee jump! She's terrified, and she ⁶ _____ (think):

'I ⁷ _____ (not enjoy) this. Why ⁸ _____ I _____ (do) it?

I'm crazy!'

3 Extension A puzzle

Read the clues and find the answer.

It takes people all over England. It sometimes goes under the sea to France. At the moment
the 18.05 is leaving Paddington Station in London. It's taking 400 people to Plymouth.

What is it? It's _____

Now think of a thing, an animal or a person and write some clues. Can your friend guess the answer?

_____

_____

Unit 5 Learning diary

Date ....

At the end of Unit 5, I can:

	Easy	Not bad	Difficult

- describe places in my town. ☐ ☐ ☐

  In the town centre there's a ....

- understand and give directions. ☐ ☐ ☐

  on the left = ... (*In my language*)

  on the right = ...

  Turn left. = ... Turn right. = ...

  Go across the square. = ...

  Go along King's Road. = ...

  Go past the chemist's. = ...

- spell these verbs in the present continuous. ☐ ☐ ☐

  sit *I'm sitting* get .... put ....

  run *I'm running* swim .... travel ....

  come .... arrive .... dance .... leave ....

- describe actions in progress at the moment. ☐ ☐ ☐

  At the moment I'm writing in my Learning Diary. I'm sitting ....

  ....

- use the two present tenses in English. ☐ ☐ ☐

  I'm .... at the moment. (*present continuous*)

  I usually .... (*present simple*)

KEY WORDS

In town

bank ....

car park ....

....

....

Unit 5 was

interesting ☐ quite interesting ☐ not very interesting ☐

Echoes of the past

1 Key vocabulary *Places*

Write the words.

1 A very tall building.

s k y s c r a p e r

2 Trafalgar .... is in London and Times .... is in New York.

..... q ....

3 The town's leaders work here.

..... o .... a .....

4 ✝

.... h

5 A small group of houses and shops. It isn't a town.

.... l ....

6 You can buy things here. It's usually outside in the street.

.... k ....

7 There are a lot of trees here.

.... s .....

8 ▉

.... t .....

9 If you want to drive a car across a river, this is necessary.

.... g .....

10 A large building where people make things (cars, for example).

.... c ....

2 *There was/were*: affirmative and negative G→ 17c

Complete the sentences. Use *There was/wasn't/were/weren't.*

Why are pictures 5 and 6 wrong?

1 .... a Roman town here 2,000 years ago.

2 .... a .... here in medieval times.

5 .... any .... in 1300.

3 .... in the garden last night.

4 .... a lot of .... in the 13th century.

6 .... any .... in the Stone Age.

32 Module 3

3 There was/were: questions and short answers 17c

Put the words in the right order and make questions. Then write true answers.

1 a / TV / night / James Bond / was / film / on / last / there ?

A: _Was there a James Bond film on TV last night?_

B: _No, there wasn't._ or _Yes, there was._

2 interesting / were / any / programmes / there ?

A: ....

....

B: ....

3 your / there / party / at / was / house / yesterday / a ?

A: ....

....

B: ....

4 letters / morning / there / this / any / for / were / you ?

A: ....

....

B: ....

5 was / a / morning / of / traffic / lot / this / there ?

A: ....

....

B: ....

4 There was/were and It was / They were

 17d

Alec had a bad dream last night. Complete his description. Use *there was, there were, it was* or *they were*.

¹ _There was_ a forest. ² _It was_ a dark, scary forest.

³ .... some people in the forest.

⁴ .... very tall, with strange clothes.

In front of me ⁵ .... a river. I wanted

to swim across, but ⁶ .... sharks in the

river. ⁷ .... silver with cruel, yellow eyes.

Suddenly, I heard a voice behind me. ⁸ ....

my mother's voice. Then I woke up.

5 Listening

What did they say?

Listen to four short conversations. Put a tick (✓) under the right answer: A, B or C.

1 How many people were there at the party?

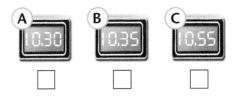

A	B	C
23	30	13
☐	☐	☐

2 What time did Paul catch the bus?

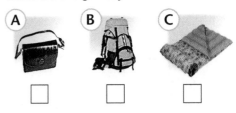

A	B	C
10.30	10.35	10.55
☐	☐	☐

3 What did the girl buy?

A	B	C
☐	☐	☐

4 What was there in the man's village?

A	B	C
☐	☐	☐

6 Extension *A map*

In your notebook, draw a map of an imaginary town. Use pictures or symbols and label the places: *river, castle, factory, town hall,* etc.

1 Present continuous and past continuous 5c, 6c

Two months ago Sally was on holiday in Biarritz. She sent this postcard to her friend Emma.

Now Sally is home and she's looking at the postcard. Write her memories. Put the sentences in the postcard into the past.

SALLY: I remember when I wrote that card!

1 *We were sitting on the beach.*

2 *The sun* _____

3 _____

4 _____

5 _____

6 _____

7 _____

Hi, Emma!

This is our first day in Biarritz. We're sitting on the beach. The sun's shining. I'm wearing my new sunglasses. I'm not thinking about school. My brother's surfing. Mum and Dad aren't arguing! We're all having a fantastic time.

Love, Sally

2 Past continuous: affirmative and negative 6a

Complete the sentences. Use the past continuous form of the verbs in the box. Then match the sentences with the pictures.

| not feel   read   not wear   get dark   ~~rain~~   listen to |

1 We didn't go for a walk because *it was raining* _____ .   Picture *F*

2 She left the beach because _____ .   Picture ____

3 He didn't hear the telephone because _____ music.   Picture ____

4 He went to the wrong door because _____ his glasses.   Picture ____

5 She didn't want to watch TV because _____ her magazine.   Picture ____

6 We didn't enjoy the boat trip because _____ very well.   Picture ____

3 Writing a report G➤ 6a

Someone stole some money from a newsagent's yesterday. A woman, Mrs Dean, saw a boy and girl in the shop. Read the conversation and complete the police officer's report. Use the past continuous form of the verbs in the box.

| wear (x 2)   carry   look at   not wear |
| ~~stand~~   ~~not buy~~ |

OFFICER: Where were they standing when you saw them?

MRS DEAN: [1] Near the door.

OFFICER: Were they buying anything?

MRS DEAN: [2] No.

OFFICER: What were they doing?

MRS DEAN: [3] Looking at magazines.

OFFICER: What was the boy wearing?

MRS DEAN: [4] Trousers and a T-shirt.

OFFICER: Was he wearing a jacket?

MRS DEAN: [5] No.

OFFICER: Was he carrying anything?

MRS DEAN: [6] Yes, a rucksack.

OFFICER: What was the girl wearing?

MRS DEAN: [7] A green anorak.

Police report

Mrs Sally Dean's statement

1 The boy and the girl _were standing near the door._

2 They _weren't buying anything._

3 They _____

4 The boy _____

5 He _____

6 He _____

7 The girl _____

4 Past continuous: questions G➤ 6b

Put the words in the right order and make questions. Then complete the conversation with the right questions.

going / you / fast / were / ?
~~going / you / where / were / ?~~
speed / doing / you / were / what / ?
your / you / mobile / using / were / ?
road / watching / were / the / you / ?
you / there / why / going / were / ?

FATHER: [1] _Where were you going?_

PETE: To Long Ashton.

FATHER: [2] _____

PETE: I was going to see a friend.

FATHER: [3] _____

PETE: No, I wasn't. I never drive fast.

FATHER: [4] _____

PETE: Oh, about 40 kilometres an hour.

FATHER: [5] _____

PETE: Yes, I was. There weren't any cars in front of me.

FATHER: [6] _____

PETE: No, I wasn't.

Sorry, Dad.

5 Extension   *A historic moment!*

Aliens came to Earth at 7.30 this morning! What was happening in your home at 7.30? Write at least four sentences.

My brother was having a shower. I was ...

_____
_____
_____
_____
_____
_____

1 Key grammar *could, couldn't* 11c

Complete the sentences. Use *could* or *couldn't* with the verbs in the box.

> go to sleep   hear   choose   ~~go out~~   play football   see

1 Judith had a lot of homework yesterday evening. She _*couldn't go out*_ .

2 Joe was standing behind two tall people at the concert. He _____ .

3 Kate was tired. She got into bed. At last she _____ .

4 Carla's hotel was near the beach. At night she _____ the sea.

5 Andy broke his leg. He _____ .

6 Fiona had a problem. Three boys wanted to go out with her. She _____ .

2 Reading *Saved!*

Read the newspaper story. Write *T* (true), *F* (false) or *?* (the answer isn't in the text).

CHRIS HINDS from Middlesbrough saw an amazing thing yesterday afternoon.

He was walking along the bank of the river Tees with his son Neil. It was a fine afternoon and they were enjoying the walk. In front of them, they could see a dog. It was sitting on the path. Chris could see that it had a broken leg.

When he and Neil went towards the dog, it tried to run away, but it couldn't, and it fell into the river.

The water was moving very fast and soon the dog was fifty metres from the bank.

Suddenly, Chris and his son saw a seal. It was swimming round the dog. When the dog's head went under the water, the seal went into action!

It pushed the dog to the river bank. Then it swam back to the middle of the river and waited. Chris ran along the bank and pulled the dog on to the path. At that moment the seal disappeared.

Chris couldn't believe his eyes. 'You only see that sort of thing in Disney films, but I saw it in real life. It happened right in front of me!' he said. 'I couldn't believe my eyes!'

1 Chris Hinds lives in Middlesbrough.   _T_

2 He was walking along the river because he wanted to find his dog.   _____

3 It was Saturday afternoon.   _____

4 The weather was good.   _____

5 The dog came towards Chris and his son.   _____

6 Chris didn't know that the dog had a broken leg.   _____

7 The dog didn't want to go into the river.   _____

8 The seal pushed the dog's head under the water.   _____

9 When Chris pulled the dog onto the path, the seal disappeared.   _____

10 The seal saved the dog's life.   _____

11 Chris and Neil were at the cinema.   _____

12 The dog's name was Lucky.   _____

3 Extension *Memories*

Think of things you can do now, but you couldn't do when you were two years old.

I couldn't play the guitar.

_____

_____

Unit 6 Learning diary

Date _____

At the end of Unit 6, I can:

	Easy	Not bad	Difficult
describe places in the past.	☐	☐	☐

In 1820 the town was quite small. There was a church, a _____

_____ .

There weren't any _____ .

	Easy	Not bad	Difficult
use *There was/were* and *It was / They were.*	☐	☐	☐

There was a castle on the hill. It was _____ .

There were two factories. They were _____ .

	Easy	Not bad	Difficult
describe actions in progress in the past.	☐	☐	☐

At 7.00 this morning I was having breakfast. I was _____ ing _____ .

At seven o'clock this morning I was having breakfast. = _____

_____ *(in my language)*

	Easy	Not bad	Difficult
use *could/couldn't* for actions that were/weren't possible in the past.	☐	☐	☐

When I was ill, I _____ to school.

Mozart was amazing. He _____ the piano when he was three years old.

KEY WORDS

Places

church _____ _____ _____

town _____ _____ _____

_____ _____ _____

_____ _____ _____

Unit 6 was

interesting ☐   quite interesting ☐   not very interesting ☐

7 Differences

STEP 1

1 Key vocabulary *Adjectives*

Think of an example for each description.

1 A very big country .... *Russia* ....
2 A small country ....
3 An expensive pastime ....
4 A cheap pastime ....
5 A long boy's name ....
6 A short girl's name ....

7 A tall building ....
8 A very old building ....
9 A new film ....
10 A fast car ....
11 A young sports star ....
12 A very slow animal ....

2 Comparatives Ⓖ→ 22a, 22b, 22c

Complete the table of adjectives and their comparative forms.

1	small	*smaller*	6	expensive	....
2	interesting	....	7	fast	....
3	famous	....	8	important	....
4	....	more exciting	9	....	older
5	cheap	....	10	easy	....

3 Comparing things and people Ⓖ→ 22a, 22b, 22c

Compare the things/people and write two sentences.
Use the adjectives in the box and their opposites.

old   tall   ~~cheap~~   difficult   fast

80 kph   112 kph

3 The cheetah is ....
   The lion is ....

> 1 **Who were the Beatles?**
> 2 **What is the theory of relativity?**

Porsche €43,500   Audi €35,000

1 The Audi is *cheaper than the Porsche* .
   The Porsche is *more expensive than the Audi* .

4 Question 1 is ....
   Question 2 is ....

Ben 1.85 m   Sophie 1.56 m

23   18

2 Ben is ....
   Sophie is ....

5 Polly is ....
   Martin is ....

4 Reading *The World Wide Web*

Read the text. Then complete the sentences with words from the text.

> In the 1960s the English science fiction writer Arthur C. Clarke said: 'In the year 2000 the world will have an enormous electronic library.'
>
> **1969** The *Internet* was born. Universities in the USA wanted to share information, so they connected their computers together and made a computer *network*. Today the Internet connects millions of computer networks together all over the world. It uses satellites and telephone lines.
>
> **1971** An American, Ray Tomlinson, invented *email* (electronic mail). Email uses the Internet. Now we can write a message and send it across the world in a few seconds. Email is a lot faster and cheaper than using the post office!
>
> **1991** An Englishman, Tim Berners-Lee, invented the *World Wide Web* (*www*).The World Wide Web is a collection of documents called *web pages*. The pages can carry words, pictures, sounds and video films. The 'Web' is an enormous library of information.
>
> **TODAY** Everyone can share information on the Internet. You can have your own *website*. There are billions of websites, and the number gets bigger every day. Arthur C. Clarke was right!

The Internet in the USA. A real spider's web!

1 A group of computers connected together is a computer <u>network</u> .

2 The .... connects lots of computer networks together.

3 The *e* in *email* means ....

4 Email is .... and .... than an ordinary letter.

5 An English scientist .... the World Wide Web.

6 *www* means ....

7 You can put words, pictures, sounds or video films on a ....

   ....

8 Your .... is your own place on the World Wide Web.

5 Word work *Computers*

Connect the parts on the right to the computer.

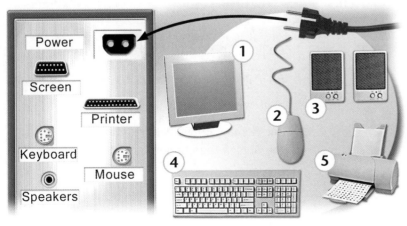

6 Extension

What's the difference?

Look at Exercise 1 again. Write at least four comparative sentences about the examples you wrote.

Russia is bigger than Spain. A Ferrari is more expensive than a Porsche.

1 Key vocabulary *Modern inventions*

Put the letters in the right order and find seven things. Then match them with the sentences (1–8).

> ~~VDD~~ glidati treelcci shrubothot
> grifed ~~yalper~~ oreest rameca
> crimewvoa swingah rhyrredia
> amniche

a   DVD player

b   ....

c   ....

d   ....

e   ....

f   ....

g   ....

h   ....

1   You can wash your clothes in this. ....

2   You can look at your photos on a computer if you use this. ....

3   You can clean your teeth with this. ....

4   You can cook your dinner in two minutes with this. ....

5   You can watch a film in your living room with this.   *a*

6   You can play your favourite music on this. ....

7   You can put your milk, butter, yoghurt and eggs in this. ....

8   You can use this after you wash your hair. ....

2 Comparatives and *as ... as ...*   23

Look at the information. Are sentences 1–10 true or false?

Annual rainfall
California 2,727 mm
Arizona   1,122 mm

Average daily sunshine (January)
Sydney   8 hours
Melbourne   9 hours

Humber Bridge (UK)   1,410 m
Golden Gate Bridge (USA) 1,280 m

Kangaroo 72 kph
Giraffe   56 kph

1   Sydney is sunnier than Melbourne.   *False.*

2   A giraffe isn't as fast as a kangaroo.   ....

3   Melbourne isn't as sunny as Sydney.   ....

4   California isn't as dry as Arizona.   ....

5   A giraffe is faster than a kangaroo.   ....

6   The Humber Bridge isn't as long as
the Golden Gate Bridge.   ....

7   California is drier than Arizona.   ....

8   A kangaroo isn't as fast as a giraffe.   ....

9   Sydney isn't as sunny as Melbourne.   ....

10   The Humber Bridge is longer than
the Golden Gate Bridge.   ....

3 Questions with *as ... as ...* G ▶ 23

Make questions and write true answers.

1 English / difficult / Chinese?

A: *Is English as difficult as Chinese?*

B: *No, it isn't.*

2 New Zealand / big / Australia?

A: ....

B: ....

3 Big Ben / tall / the Eiffel Tower?

A: ....

B: ....

4 a kilo of balloons / heavy / a kilo of onions?

A: ....

B: ....

5 a kilometre / long / a mile?

A: ....

B: ....

4 Spelling

Can you spell the comparative form of these adjectives?

1 happy   *happier*   5 hot ....

2 nice ....   6 friendly ....

3 sunny ....   7 big ....

4 easy ....   8 noisy ....

Hi, everyone!

This place is paradise, so I'm not coming home. I like .... (name of your town/village), but it isn't as ...

Write to me soon.

Love, ...

5 Listening   *Me and my dog*

🔊 Listen to Sadie talking about Lisa and Sam, the dog. Circle the right answer: a, b or c.

1 Sadie and Lisa

  a always argue.

  b like arguing.

  ⓒ had an argument today.

2 At the moment Sadie

  a isn't very happy.

  b isn't fed up.

  c is having an argument with Lisa.

3 Sadie thinks

  a dogs aren't as nice as people.

  b people are awful.

  c people aren't as nice as dogs.

4 Sam

  a is always in a good mood

  b is Lisa's dog.

  c doesn't like Sadie's parents.

5 Sadie thinks Lisa

  a is never in a bad mood.

  b is funnier than her other friends.

  c isn't as funny as her other friends.

6 Sadie

  a is going to send Lisa an email.

  b doesn't like talking to Lisa.

  c wants to be friends with Lisa again.

6 Extension

Write a letter

Imagine you're on Richie Sowa's island. You want to stay there. In your notebook, write a short letter to your family. Say why you aren't coming home.

1 Possessive 's (G) 26a, 26b, 22d

Write two sentences for each picture. Use the possessive 's and the comparative form of the adjectives.

1 Zoe / expensive / Ann

Zoe's hairdryer is more expensive than Ann's.

Ann / expensive / Zoe

Ann's hairdryer isn't

2 Kathy / interesting / Luke

....

Luke / interesting / Kathy

....

3 Megan / good / Fiona

....

Fiona / good / Megan

....

4 Jenny / big / Mike

....

Mike / big / Jenny

....

2 Dialogue completion *Possessive pronouns*  27a, 27c

Dan's talking to the coach driver after a school trip. Complete the conversation. Choose the right sentences from the list (a–i).

- a I think it's mine.
- b It isn't mine.
- c Mine are bigger than his.
- d And whose is this money?
- e Hers are red.
- f Perhaps they're his.
- g Have you got €20?
- h Whose are these trainers?
- i My feet aren't as big as that!

DRIVER: Whose are these red sunglasses?

DAN: I think they're Helen's. [1] *e*

DRIVER: [2] ...... Are they yours?

DAN: You must be joking! [3] ...... Luke's got big feet. [4] ......

DRIVER: And what about this CD?

DAN: I don't know. [5] ......

DRIVER: [6] ...... Look! €20.

DAN: [7] ......

DRIVER: Are you sure it's yours?

3 Extension *I, me, my, mine* (G) 28a, 27a

Can you complete the four lists?

Subject pronoun (*I like music.*)	I	you	he	she	it	we	you	they
Object pronoun (*She likes me.*)	me	you	....	....	....	....	....	....
Possessive adjective (*my sister*)	my	your	....	....	....	....	....	....
Possessive pronoun (*It's mine.*)	mine	....	....	....	....	....	....	....

Unit 7 Learning diary

Date _____

At the end of Unit 7, I can:

	Easy	Not bad	Difficult
use adjectives in English.	☐	☐	☐

an expensive computer   a _____ car   a _____

| compare two things. | ☐ | ☐ | ☐ |

A Mercedes is very expensive. It's _____ *than a skidoo.*

Joe is 16 and Sadie is 13. Joe is _____ *than Sadie.*

The Nile is longer than the Mississippi. = _____

_____ *(in my language)*

Love is more important than money. = _____

_____

	Easy	Not bad	Difficult
describe similarities and differences using *as ... as*.	☐	☐	☐

Are lions _____ *fast* _____ *cheetahs?*

English isn't _____ *difficult* _____ *Japanese.*

Tennis isn't as interesting as baseball. = _____

_____

	Easy	Not bad	Difficult
talk about people's possessions.	☐	☐	☐

That isn't my pen. It's yours. = _____

Where's Lisa? This pen is hers. = _____

Where's Ben? This pen is his. = _____

This camera isn't ours. It's theirs. = _____

It's mine. = _____   It's Lisa's. = _____

KEY WORDS

Adjectives

big _____   _____

_____   _____

_____   _____

_____   _____

Modern inventions

digital camera _____   _____

_____   _____

_____   _____

Unit 7 was

interesting ☐   quite interesting ☐   not very interesting ☐

8 Our incredible world

1 Key vocabulary *How long is it?*

What are these people thinking? Write questions with *How* + adjective + *is it?*

| long | old | ~~tall~~ | high | far | dangerous |

1 *How tall is it?*

2 _____

3 _____

4 _____

5 _____

6 _____

2 Adjectives: comparatives and superlatives (G) 22a, 22b, 22c

Complete the table.

1	long	*longer*	the longest
2	_____	bigger	the biggest
3	difficult	more difficult	_____
4	easy	easier	_____
5	powerful	_____	the most powerful
6	hot	_____	_____
7	important	_____	_____

3 Superlatives

Complete the sentences. Use the superlative form of the adjectives in the box.

| lazy | long | heavy | ~~large~~ |
| popular | tall | big |

1 Jupiter is ___the largest___ planet in the solar system.

2 A giraffe can be 5.8 metres tall. It's ___the___ _____ animal in the world.

3 A blue whale can be 30 metres long and can weigh 150 tonnes. It's _____ and _____ animal in the world.

4 _____ animal in the world is the koala. It sleeps for 18–22 hours a day!

5 Chloe is _____ girl's name in Britain.

6 The First World Hotel in Malaysia has got 6,300 rooms. It's _____ hotel in the world.

4 Reading *The Grand Canyon*

Read the text and answer the questions.

Visit the

Grand Canyon

North west Arizona, USA

THE COLORADO RIVER CREATED THIS CANYON SIX MILLION YEARS AGO.

- It's 446 km long.
- It's 16–29 kilometres wide.
- It's 1,500–1,800 metres deep.

WALK, RIDE A HORSE, OR TAKE A RAFT

- You can walk from the top of the canyon to the bottom, and then back to the top (2 days).
- You can go through the canyon on a raft (2 weeks).

WEAR THE RIGHT CLOTHES

It's hotter and drier at the bottom than at the top.
There's sometimes a difference of 26°C.
It's 50°C at the bottom in the summer!

ENJOY THE ADVENTURE AND THE MYSTERY

You can touch rocks that are two billion years old.
You can learn about the mysterious caves.

1 Where is the Grand Canyon?
   It's in ....

2 What can you see at the bottom of the canyon?
   ....

3 How old is the canyon?
   ....

4 How long is it?
   ....

5 How wide is it at the widest point?
   ....

6 How deep is it at the deepest point?
   ....

7 What can you do if you've got two free weeks?
   ....

8 Is it hotter at the bottom than at the top?
   ....

9 How hot is it at the bottom in the summer?
   ....

10 How old are some of the rocks?
   ....

5 Extension *Puzzles*

Write the answers.

1 Tom is 1.8 m. Rick is shorter than Ryan. Ryan is 1.7 m.

   a Who's taller than Ryan? ....
   b Who's the shortest? ....

2 Mark's bike cost €300. Kate's bike was cheaper, but it was more expensive than Peter's.

   a Was Peter's bike cheaper than Mark's?
   ....

   b Whose bike was the most expensive?
   ....

3 St Paul's Cathedral in London gets a million visitors a year. The Tower of London gets 2.5 million, but it isn't as popular as the London Eye.
Which place is the most popular? ....

The London Eye

Word work *A trip*

Find the right words and phrases in the word square. Then complete the list.

```
R O N X T O L J K
E E Y D A S T A Y
L J C O S T H M G
A C O U P L E O F
T R A I E E M S R
I N C E N W E L A
V M H A D F P A N
E A E S O C A M P
S O T E K A R J N
V I S I T T K D I
```

1 Jack doesn't want to _____ a lot of old churches. (5)   *visit*

2 This phrase means 'two or three'. (3 words: 1, 6, 2) _____

3 Kate's going to _____ some time in London. (5) _____

4 I never _____ in bed all day. (4) _____

5 The people in your family are your _____ . (9) _____

6 Disneyworld is a _____ . (2 words: 5, 4) _____

7 This is a sort of bus. (5) _____

8 I'm going to take my tent, so I can _____ . (4) _____

2 *going to*: affirmative (G)► 8

What are their plans? Write sentences with *going to* and the verbs in the box.

> play   camp   have   buy   clean   ~~go~~

1 I'm going to go on the roller coaster .

2 Mike _____ .

3 Maggie _____ .

4 They _____ .

5 Sally and Leo _____ .

6 I _____ .

3 *going to*: negative (G) ➤ 8

Write sentences. Use the negative form of *going to*.

1 A shop assistant is showing Jenny a top, but Jenny doesn't like it.

   She *isn't going to buy it*   .

2 There's a horror film on TV tonight. Cassie and Fran don't like scary films.

   They _____ .

3 Ryan's at a party. He wants to dance with Lucy or Zoe, but the two girls don't like him.

   LUCY: We _____ .

4 Gemma's a vegetarian. She's in the school canteen. She can have chicken, or pasta and vegetables.

   She _____ .

5 Mark usually does his homework after dinner. But tonight there's a football match on TV.

   He _____ .

6 Luke wants to go to London. The coach costs €25. The train costs €105!

   LUKE: I _____ .

4 *going to*: questions (G) ➤ 8

Put the words in the right order and make questions.
Match them with the situations.

going / do / we / what / are / to ?
to / you / it / going / buy / are ?
am / wear / to / I / going / what ?
you / who / going / invite / to / are ?
~~to / what / see / are / going / you~~ ?
going / have / what / to / you / are ?

1 Chris can see his friend Guy outside the cinema.

   CHRIS: *What are you going to see?* _____

2 Emily's looking at the menu at the café. Beth's speaking to her.

   BETH: _____

3 Polly's writing a list of names for her party. Her friend Sarah is speaking to her.

   SARAH: _____

4 Rick's looking at a CD in a music shop. His friend Tim is speaking to him.

   TIM: _____

5 Tom and Helen are at the door of their flat. But the door's locked and they haven't got a key.

   TOM: _____

6 Chloe's looking at the clothes in her wardrobe.

   CHLOE: _____

5 Extension

What are your plans?

Choose three of these people and imagine their plans. Write a sentence for each person. (You can write about other people if you like.)

A The manager of Real Madrid Football Club
B The leader of your country
C The head teacher of your school
D The manager of national television

B I'm going to give €1,000 to every teenager.

_____

_____

_____

_____

_____

_____

_____

_____

_____

1 Irregular comparatives and superlatives 22d

Complete the sentences with the words in the box.

the worst	~~better~~	the best	worse

1 James is __better than__ Nina, but he's

.... Alice and Dan.

2 Dan is .... Alice, but he's

.... James and ....

3 Nina is .... Alice, Dan and James.

She's ....

4 Alice is .... Nina, James and Dan.

She's ....

James   Dan   Nina   Alice

2 Listening *Who got the best score?*

a 🔊 Listen to Emma and Andy talking about a computer game called *Commando*. Complete the score card.

b Read the sentences. Are they true or false?

1 Emma's score was worse than her brother's. ....

2 Andy's score wasn't as good as Dave's. ....

3 Dave didn't get the best score. ....

4 The worst score was 4,565. ....

5 Andy got a better score than Emma's brother. ....

6 Andy's mum got the best score of all. ....

COMMANDO

score card ▼

Name	Score
....	4,565
....	4,620
Andy's mum	4,625
....	4,560
....	4,590

3 Extension *Your preferences*

What's your opinion? Write your answers to these questions.

1 What's the best place in the world? ....

2 What's your most important possession? ....

3 Who's the nicest person in the world? ....

4 What's the worst month of the year? ....

5 What's the best day of the week? ....

6 What's the most interesting subject at school? ....

7 What's the best programme on television? ....

8 What's the worst programme on television? ....

9 What's the most boring sport? ....

Unit 8 Learning diary

Date _____

At the end of Unit 8, I can:

	Easy	Not bad	Difficult

- describe dimensions. ☐ ☐ ☐

  The river is 500 kilometres _____ . The Sun is millions of years _____ .

  The Empire State Building is 381 metres _____ . Matt is 1.72 metres _____ .

- ask questions with *How* + adjective. ☐ ☐ ☐

  How _____ is the River Thames? _____ are the Pyramids?

- compare one thing with the rest of a group. ☐ ☐ ☐

  The Nile is the longest river in _____ .

  Mount Everest is _____ .

  The Mercedes CLK/LM is _____ .

  The most difficult subject at school is _____ .

- talk about plans and intentions using *going to*. ☐ ☐ ☐

  Kate is _____ travel across the USA with her cousin.

  They _____ visit the Six Flags theme park.

  I'm going to _____ next weekend.

- remember the comparative and superlative of *good* and *bad*. ☐ ☐ ☐

	Comparative	Superlative
good	_____	_____
bad	_____	_____

KEY WORDS

Expressions with *How ...?*

How long? _____

_____ _____

_____ _____

_____ _____

Going on a trip

bus _____

camera _____

_____ _____

_____ _____

Unit 8 was

interesting ☐ quite interesting ☐ not very interesting ☐

9 Looking ahead

1 *will, won't* 7a

Complete the sentences with *'ll* or *won't*.

1 It _'ll_ be for me.

2 A: Hurry up! You _____ be late for school.

B: I _____ be late! It's only ten past eight.

3 A: I don't want to go through the city. We _____ get lost.

B: We _____ get lost. I've got a street map.

4 Let's ask her. She _____ know.

5 You _____ enjoy it. It's a great film.

6 They _____ win. They aren't playing well.

2 Predictions 7a, 7c

Read Anna's horoscope and complete the sentences. Use *will/'ll* or *won't* with the verbs in the box.

meet ~~argue~~ get change be (x 2) have help

GEMINI
May 21st – June 21st

You'll disagree with a friend at the beginning of the week and you'll feel sad. You'll talk to other friends about the problem, but they won't listen. But be optimistic! Your positive attitude will help you. Things will be different at the end of the week and you'll feel better. You'll get an exciting phone call. A new and interesting person will come into your life. Friday will probably be the best day of the week.

1 Anna _will argue_ with a friend.

2 She _____ a good time in the first part of the week.

3 Her other friends _____ her.

4 The situation _____ at the end of the week.

5 She _____ a phone call.

6 It _____ an ordinary phone call.

7 She _____ a new and interesting person.

8 Friday _____ probably _____ a good day.

3 Reading *Our changing planet*

Look at the maps and read the text. Are the sentences true or false? Correct the false sentences.

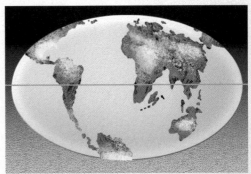
Our planet in 50 million years' time

250 MILLION YEARS AGO THERE WAS ONE BIG CONTINENT ON EARTH. Scientists called it Pangaea. Very, very slowly, Pangaea divided, and today there are five separate continents. But the shape of our world is changing because the continents move about ten centimetres every year.

So what will our planet be like 50 million years from now? Scientists think that the Atlantic Ocean will get bigger and the Pacific Ocean will get smaller. The Mediterranean Sea will disappear. Europe and Africa will join together. North and South America will separate, and Australia will move north. In Africa, the Great Rift Valley will get longer and East Africa will become an island. Alaska and Russia will join together.

What will happen after that? Some scientists believe that, in 250 million years' time, the five different continents won't exist. There will be one big continent again – a new Pangaea!

... and in 250 million years' time

1 The shape of our world will always be the same.
   False. The shape of our world will change.

2 The oceans will all get smaller.

3 In 50 million years' time the Earth won't be very different.

4 The Mediterranean Sea won't exist.

5 Europe and Africa won't be separate continents.

6 Australia will move nearer to Asia.

7 Africa will become an island.

8 250 million years from now, there won't be five different continents.

4 Extension *A horoscope*

Choose a star sign and write a horoscope. Write at least three predictions.

| Aries | Taurus | Gemini | Cancer | Leo | Virgo | Libra | Scorpio | Sagittarius | Capricorn | Aquarius | Pisces |

ARIES – You'll have a difficult day tomorrow.

1 Key vocabulary *Important events*

Complete the sentences with the phrases in the box.

> leave school   fell in love   taking her maths exam   passed her exams   ~~got married~~
> failed her maths exam   goes abroad   going out with   get a new job

1 My aunt met my uncle when they were both 19. They _____got married_____ when they were 21.

2 Ella worked hard at school last year and she _____ .

3 Students in England can _____ when they're 16.

4 My father's a taxi driver, but he doesn't enjoy it. He wants to _____ .

5 My grandfather never _____ for his holidays. He always stays in England.

6 Martha _____ . She only got 27%.

7 A: Has Tim got a girlfriend?
    B: Yes, he's _____ Leila.

8 Fran's _____ this morning. She's very nervous.

9 Danny and Helen _____ when they were 23 and they got married two years later.

2 Listening *A holiday in Egypt*

🔊 Listen to the holiday advertisement and complete the text. Then label the pictures.

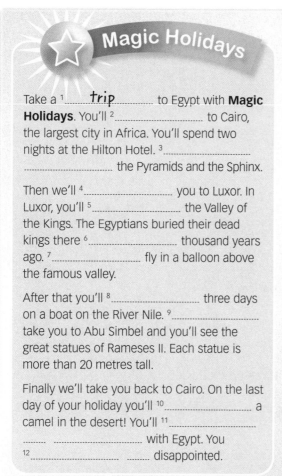

Magic Holidays

Take a ¹ ____trip____ to Egypt with **Magic Holidays**. You'll ² _____ to Cairo, the largest city in Africa. You'll spend two nights at the Hilton Hotel. ³ _____ _____ the Pyramids and the Sphinx.

Then we'll ⁴ _____ you to Luxor. In Luxor, you'll ⁵ _____ the Valley of the Kings. The Egyptians buried their dead kings there ⁶ _____ thousand years ago. ⁷ _____ fly in a balloon above the famous valley.

After that you'll ⁸ _____ three days on a boat on the River Nile. ⁹ _____ take you to Abu Simbel and you'll see the great statues of Rameses II. Each statue is more than 20 metres tall.

Finally we'll take you back to Cairo. On the last day of your holiday you'll ¹⁰ _____ a camel in the desert! You'll ¹¹ _____ _____ with Egypt. You ¹² _____ disappointed.

A   *The Pyramids*

C _____

E _____

B _____

D _____

3 Questions with *will* 7b

Put the words in the right order and make questions. Then look at the dice and write the short answers. 1, 2 and 3 on the dice mean *Yes*. 4, 5 and 6 mean *No*.

> Will I have an exciting life?

1 life / I / have / will / exciting / an ?

A: Will I have an exciting life?

B: Yes, you will.

2 on / be / one / day / television / will / I ?

A: ....

B: ....

3 I / of / have / lot / girlfriends / will / a ?

A: ....

B: ....

4 Sarah / with / fall / love / me / will / in ?

A: ....

B: ....

5 be / exams / my / easy / will ?

A: ....

B: ....

6 will / the / biology / fail / I / exam ?

A: ....

B: ....

4 More questions with *will* 7b

These people are worried. What are they thinking? Write two questions with *will*.

1 Diana's French pen friend is coming to stay with her for the first time.

a what / she / be like?

What will she be like?

b she / happy here?

....

2 Tony's got a maths exam tomorrow.

a what / the questions / be like?

....

b they / difficult?

....

3 Harry's DVD player is broken. He's taking it to the shop.

a how much / it / cost?

....

b it / expensive?

....

4 Sandra's going home after a party. It's very late.

a what / my parents / say?

....

b they / angry?

....

5 Extension *A holiday advertisement*

Look again at Exercise 2. In your notebook, write a holiday advertisement for your country or your region. (Think of another place if you like.)

Come to ... this summer. You'll see ...
We'll take you to ...

1 Key vocabulary *Future time expressions*

Write the missing time expressions.

1 on Tuesday	<u>on Wednesday</u>	on Thursday
2 in July	in August	....
3 tomorrow morning	....	tomorrow evening
4 this afternoon	....	tonight
5	on Sunday afternoon	on Sunday evening
6 last month	this month	....
7 last year	....	next year

2 Present continuous used for the future 5d

It's now Friday afternoon. Look at Rachel's diary and complete the sentences about her weekend. Use the present continuous and the words in the box.

> ~~this evening~~   tomorrow night   tomorrow afternoon
> tomorrow evening   tomorrow morning   tonight

● FRIDAY

    7.30 Cinema with Louise
        Sleep at Louise's house

● SATURDAY

    10.00 Go shopping with Charlotte
    3.00 Meet Rob and Louise in town
    8.00 Party at Lucy's. Home late!

---

1 Rachel<u>'s going to the cinema</u> with Louise <u>this evening</u> . (*go*)

2 She .... at Louise's house .... (*sleep*)

3 She .... with Charlotte .... (*go*)

4 Rob and Louise .... her .... (*meet*)

5 She .... (*go*)

6 She .... home late .... (*get*)

3 Questions about arrangements

Look at the answers and complete the questions about Rachel. Use *When, Where* or *Who.*

1 she / go / cinema?

  A: <u>When's she going to the cinema?</u>

  B: This evening.

2 she / sleep tonight?

  A: ....

  B: At Louise's house.

3 go shopping / with Rachel?

  A: ....

  B: Charlotte.

4 Rob and Louise / meet her?

  A: ....

  B: In town.

5 have / party / on Saturday?

  A: ....

  B: Lucy.

4 Extension *The President's diary*

Imagine you're the president of the USA. What are you doing next week? In your notebook write at least three sentences.

On Monday I'm visiting the NASA Space Centre at Cape Canaveral, in Florida.

Unit 9 Learning diary

Date _____

At the end of Unit 9, I can:

	Easy	Not bad	Difficult

- remember positive and negative adjectives. ☐ ☐ ☐

  lucky, unlucky, optimistic, _____ .

- use verbs describing exams. ☐ ☐ ☐

  take an exam = _____ *(in my language)*

  pass an exam = _____

  fail an exam = _____

- talk about events in the future using *will* and *won't*. ☐ ☐ ☐

  I'll be _____ years old on my next birthday.

  I _____ leave school in _____ *(year)*.

  Matt _____ win the race on Saturday. He _____ be second.

- ask and answer questions about the future using *will*. ☐ ☐ ☐

  When _____ you be eighteen? In _____ *(year)*.

  _____ I be happy and healthy? Yes, _____ . No, _____ .

- use the present continuous to talk about future arrangements. ☐ ☐ ☐

  Joe and Sadie _____ tennis after school tomorrow.

  I _____ next weekend.

KEY WORDS

Important events		Future time expressions	
fall in love	_____	next month	_____
_____	_____	_____	_____
_____	_____	_____	_____
_____	_____	_____	_____

Unit 9 was

interesting ☐   quite interesting ☐   not very interesting ☐

10 Some ketchup, please!

STEP 1

1 Key vocabulary *Food and drink*

Choose the right word.

1 You can't drink ___*rice*___ . (*fruit juice / rice / milk*)

2 There isn't any meat in a _____ . (*beefburger / sausage / baked potato*)

3 Could I have some _____ with my beefburger? (*salad / fruit / ice cream*)

4 _____ can be red or white. (*tomatoes / peas / grapes*)

5 Would you like a cup of tea and a _____ ? (*chip / potato / biscuit*)

6 Do you want any _____ in your tea? (*cheese / sugar / bread*)

7 We're having chicken _____ for lunch. (*soup / sauce / juice*)

8 Sadie's a vegetarian. She never eats _____ . (*rice / veggieburgers / sausages*)

9 Would you like some _____ on your fish? (*sugar / water / sauce*)

10 _____ are my favourite vegetables. (*veggieburgers / peas / grapes*)

11 Jack loves meat. He ate four _____ at the barbecue. (*potatoes / beefburgers / biscuits*)

12 Robbie doesn't drink _____ . He's only two. (*coffee / milk / fruit juice*)

2 Countable and uncountable nouns G→ 18a, 18b

Put the words in the right lists.

> ~~grapes~~ ~~bread~~ ~~egg~~ sauce biscuits rice veggieburger vegetables baked potato sausage peas sugar

a/an	**some +** **plural noun**	**some +** **uncountable noun**
an egg	some grapes	some bread
....	....	....
....	....	....
....	....	....

3 a/an and some G→ 18a, 18b

Complete the text, using *a/an* or *some*.

Last night Pete cooked [1] ___*a*___ meal for his friend Sarah. He decided to make a risotto. He cooked [2] _____ rice and he added [3] _____ cheese and [4] _____ peas. He found [5] _____ beefburger, [6] _____ apple and [7] _____ grapes in the fridge, and he added them too. The rice was a bit dry, so he added [8] _____ fruit juice. Sarah really enjoyed the meal. 'That was [9] _____ brilliant risotto, Pete. Thank you. Have you got the recipe?' she said.

4 Could I ... ? (G)→ 15a, 15b

Write polite questions with *Could I ...?*

1 You're at the cinema. You want two tickets.

   Could I have two tickets, please?

2 You're at a café. You want some lemonade.

3 You haven't got a dictionary. You want to use your teacher's.

4 You're on a train with your friend's family. You want to sit by the window.

5 You're phoning the President of the USA. His secretary answers the phone.

6 You're in the school canteen. You want some pasta.

5 Would you like ...? I'd like ... (G)→ 15a, 15b

a Put the sentences in the right order (1–4) and make four conversations.

1 [2] Yes, please.
   [4] I'd like some fruit juice, please.
   [1] Would you like a drink?
   [3] Water or fruit juice?

2 [ ] Would you like some ketchup with it?
   [ ] Have a beefburger.
   [ ] Oh, thanks.
   [ ] Yes, please.

3 [ ] Could I have a veggieburger?
   [ ] What would you like?
   [ ] No, thanks.
   [ ] Would you like a baked potato with it?

4 [ ] Thanks.
   [ ] Would you like a baked potato?
   [ ] Here you are.
   [ ] Yes, please.

b Now complete these conversations with *I'd like* or *Would you like*.

5 A: *Would you like* some soup?

   B: Yes, please. _____ some bread too.

   A: _____ some butter with it?

   B: No, thanks.

6 A: _____ a drink?

   B: Yes, please.

   A: What _____ ?

   B: _____ some fruit juice, please.

6 Extension *Be polite!*

Nick and Sarah aren't very polite. Write the conversation again, using more polite sentences.

NICK:	What do you want?	1	*What would you like?*
SARAH:	I want some sausages.	2	*I'd*
NICK:	Two or three?	3	_____ ?
SARAH:	Two.	4	_____
NICK:	A baked potato?	5	_____ ?
SARAH:	Yes, and give me some ketchup.	6	*Yes, please, and* _____ ?

1 *How much/many?* G→ 20b, 20c

Complete the questions with *How much* or *How many*. Then choose the right answers from the box.

> eight   six tonnes   two hundred and fifty   six hundred thousand
> 160 litres   four hundred   ~~six hundred and forty thousand~~

1 A: _How many_ elephants are there in the world?

   B: _Six hundred and forty thousand._

2 A: _____ elephants are there in Africa?

   B: _____

3 A: _____ water do they drink a day?

   B: _____

4 A: _____ kilos of food do they eat a day?

   B: _____

5 A: _____ does an African elephant weigh?

   B: _____

6 A: _____ kilos can an adult elephant carry?

   B: _____

7 A: _____ babies does the average elephant have?

   B: _____

2 What's the reply?

Complete the conversations. Circle a, b or c.

1 Could I have some rice, please?
   a How many would you like?
   b How much would you like? (circled)
   c No, thanks.

2 I haven't got any money.
   a Yes, please.
   b How many do you need?
   c How much do you need?

3 Do you like my new trainers?
   a Yes. Here you are.
   b Yes, I do. How much did they cost?
   c No, thanks.

4 Could I have some sausages, please?
   a I don't want any sausages, thanks.
   b How many would you like?
   c How much would you like?

5 I think I'll have a glass of water.
   a How many do you want?
   b Sure. Help yourself.
   c What would you like to drink?

6 She's got lots of brothers and sisters.
   a Has she got many brothers?
   b How much has she got?
   c How many has she got?

3 Listening   *The average British man*

🔊 Listen to the information about the average man in Britain. Choose the right words or numbers.

1 The average man in Britain _weighs_ 3.3 kilos when he's born.   (*weighs / can carry / eats*)

2 He leaves school when he's _____ (*16 / 17 / 18*)

3 He _____ for 42 hours a week.   (*sleeps / works / studies*)

4 He _____ for 3½ hours.   (*works / sleeps / watches TV*)

5 His wife is _____ younger than him.   (*four years / a year / two years*)

6 He dies at the age of _____ .   (*72 / 73 / 78*)

4 Reading *The human brain*

Read the text and answer the questions.

Our brains are approximately 16 centimetres long and 14 centimetres wide – about a quarter of the size of a football. A man's brain weighs about 1.4 kilos and a woman's about 1.3 kilos. But that doesn't mean that men are more intelligent than women!

Did you know that 80% of your brain is water? But don't worry, because you've got 100 billion powerful brain cells. Your brain is a very clever machine. It sends millions of messages to every part of your body every second. When you touch a hot cooker, your brain sends a message to your fingers and you move your hand immediately. These messages travel at 580 kilometres an hour.

All this work takes a lot of energy. In fact, your brain uses 20% of your energy. It works for 24 hours a day and never gets tired. But, like you, your brain needs food, and it uses about 35 litres of blood every hour.

Will you remember all this information? Well, it's in your brain now, and your brain can hold more information than a million encyclopaedias!

1 Is your brain as big as a football?   *No, it isn't.*

2 How much does a woman's brain weigh?   ....

3 Is a woman's brain as heavy as a man's?   ....

4 How much of your brain is water?   ....

5 How many messages does your brain send every second?   ....

6 How fast do the messages travel?   ....

7 What 'food' does the brain use?   ....

8 Is there more information in your brain than in an encyclopaedia?   ....

5 Extension *Use your brain!*

Which shape is the odd one out?   ....

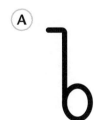 A   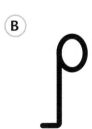 B    C    D    E

1 Affirmative sentences with *a lot of* 20a

Write two sentences about each person, using the words in the two boxes. Use *a lot of* in the second sentence.

> very healthy   very popular at school
> ~~very unhealthy~~   crazy about computers

> fast food   friends   fruit and vegetables
> computer magazines

1 Adam 's very unhealthy. He

   eats a lot of

2 Joanna _____

_____

3 Pauline _____

_____

4 Steve _____

_____

2 Negative sentences with *much/many*

Make sentences. Use *much* or *many*.  20b, 20c

1 Luke / not eat / healthy food
   Luke doesn't eat much healthy food.

2 Emma / not get / exercise

_____

3 Helen / not eat / beefburgers

_____

4 Jack / not have / problems

_____

5 Mark / not spend / time watching television

_____

3 Questions with *much/many* 20b, 20c

Complete the questions with *much* or *many*. Then write true answers.

1 A: Do you get ___much___ homework at the weekend?
   B: Yes, I do. or No, I don't.

2 A: Do you spend _____ time on the Internet?
   B: _____

3 A: Have you got _____ computer games?
   B: _____

4 A: Do you get _____ exercise?
   B: _____

5 A: Are there _____ fast food restaurants in your town?
   B: _____

4 Extension   *What sort of people are they?*

Write more sentences about these people.

1 She does a lot of sport.

_____

2 He's crazy about his work.

_____

3 He doesn't get much fresh air.

_____

Unit 10 Learning diary

Date _____

At the end of Unit 10, I can:

	Easy	Not bad	Difficult

- use countable and uncountable nouns. ☐ ☐ ☐

  Countable: *a potato*   a _____   a _____   an _____

  Uncountable: *some sauce*   some _____   some _____

- offer people food and drink. ☐ ☐ ☐

  Would you _____ some sausages?   Would _____ a cup of coffee?
  _____ some salad?

  What would you like? = _____ *(in my language)*

  Would you like some salad? = _____

- say what you would like and ask for things politely. ☐ ☐ ☐

  Jack would _____ some pasta.   I _____ some soup, please.

  I'd like some soup. = _____

  Could I _____ some bread, please?   _____ I have a biscuit?

  Could I have some soup? = _____

- Use *a lot of, much* and *many*. ☐ ☐ ☐

  How _____ sleep do you get?   How _____ CDs have you got?

  I eat a lot of _____ .   I don't eat much _____ .

  I don't eat many _____ .

KEY WORDS

Things to eat
Countable nouns

grapes   _____
beefburger   _____
_____   _____
_____   _____
_____   _____

Uncountable nouns

bread   _____
_____   _____
_____   _____
_____   _____
_____   _____

Things to drink
Uncountable nouns

water
_____
_____
_____
_____

Unit 10 was		
interesting ☐	quite interesting ☐	not very interesting ☐

STEP 1

1 can/can't: possibility G→ 11a

Complete the conversations. Use *can* or *can't* and the words in the box.

> awful   my key   isn't far   in a maths lesson   that window

1 A: _____Can_____ we walk to the town centre from here?

 B: Yes, of course we _____ . It _____
 _____ .

2 A: Oh, no! I _____ find _____ .
 What _____ we do?

 B: Perhaps we _____ open _____ .

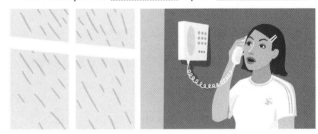

3 A: I _____ speak to you now. I'm _____
 _____ .

 B: OK. _____ you phone me later?

4 A: The weather's _____ . We
 _____ play tennis.

 B: I know. You _____ come to my house
 if you like.

2 can/can't: permission G→ 11a

a Make questions with *Can*, asking for permission.

1 You want to use your friend's DVD player.

Can I use your DVD player?

2 You want to have sky surfing lessons.

_____

3 You want to have a dog for your birthday.

_____

4 You want to paint your room red.

_____

5 You want to go to the cinema this evening.

_____

6 You and your friend want to play snooker.

_____

b Match the questions in 2a with the answers.

a   We'll see. Do you really want another pet?
b   No, sorry. It's broken.
c   Yes, OK. What are you going to see?

d   Yes, of course you can. The balls are in the cupboard.
e   No, you can't. It's too expensive, and it's dangerous.
f   What about blue?

1 b   2 _____   3 _____   4 _____   5 _____   6 _____

3 Reading *Notices*

Match the sentences with the notices.

A — ST JOHN'S BEACH — Dangerous rocks Do not go into the water !

B — SOUTH BRENT PARK — Gates close at 10 pm

C — TODAY'S BARGAIN Buy two computer games for the price of one!

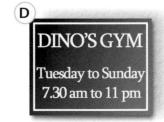

D — DINO'S GYM — Tuesday to Sunday 7.30 am to 11 pm

E — EXETER INTERNET CAFÉ — Pay at the desk before you use the computers

F — NO DOGS NO RADIOS ON THE BEACH

G — LANGLEY SPORTS CENTRE — Open 7 days a week 8 am — 9pm

H — DANGER! WILD BEARS — Do not leave food outside your tent

1 You mustn't stay here after ten o'clock.   *B*

2 There are dangerous animals here, so you must be careful.   ....

3 There are computers here, but you can't buy them.   ....

4 You can swim in the sea here.   ....

5 You can get some exercise here every day of the week.   ....

6 You mustn't swim here.   ....

4 *must, mustn't* G ▸ 12

Match sentences 1–6 with sentences a–f. Complete a–f with *must* or *mustn't*.

1 Which colour do you want?   *d*   a You _____ see it.

2 It isn't important.   ....   b You _____ eat it!

3 I think it's going to rain.   ....   c You _____ worry.

4 We're late.   ....   d You *must* choose.

5 It's a fantastic film.   ....   e We _____ hurry.

6 That fish isn't fresh.   ....   f We _____ forget the umbrella.

5 Extension *My club*

Imagine you want to start a new club. Think of a name for it and write at least three rules.

The Crazy Club: Members must wear red and yellow socks.
When a member meets another member they must both stand on one leg.

----

1 Key vocabulary *Verbs of action*

Complete the sentences. Use the right form of the verbs in the box.

get out of ~~walk~~ run after run away get into climb follow move touch

1 There weren't any buses or taxis, so we ___walked___ to the station.

2 When I arrived at the bus stop, the bus was leaving. I _____ it, but I couldn't catch it.

3 Don't _____ the cooker. It's very hot.

4 I saw my cat in the middle of the road. I tried to catch it, but it _____ and _____ a tree.

5 I don't know where the Youth Hostel is, but we can _____ the *YH* signs.

6 Lisa can't find her hamster. It _____ its cage last night and disappeared.

7 I can't _____ the house, because I haven't got a key.

8 Don't _____ ! There's a snake in front of you.

2 Advice: *should/shouldn't* 13a

Give advice to the people in the pictures. Complete the sentences with *should* or *shouldn't* and the verbs in the box.

bring walk go read follow go across get ~~use~~

1 You _should use_ the bridge.

You _____ the road there.

2 You _____ by car.

You _____ the bus.

3 You _____ there. It's dangerous.

You _____ the path.

4 You _____ your dog to the beach.

You _____ that notice.

3 Good advice (G)→ 13a

For each situation, give some good advice. Use *should* and *shouldn't*.

1 You __should__ always try to help your friends.

2 You _____ wash grapes before you eat them.

3 You _____ get angry when you disagree with a friend.

4 You _____ climb a mountain in bad weather.

5 You _____ be kind to animals.

6 You _____ eat a lot of fast food.

7 You _____ get lots of exercise.

8 You _____ touch a poison arrow frog.

9 You _____ take some warm clothes when you go on holiday to England.

10 You _____ listen to bad advice.

4 Listening *What should I do?*

🎙 Tanya has got a problem with her boyfriend, Danny. She's talking to three friends. Listen and complete the sentences. Circle the right answer: a, b or c.

1 Danny
   a wasn't on the bus this morning.
   b phoned Tanya at the weekend.
   c didn't speak to Tanya at the weekend.

2 Tanya
   a doesn't want any advice.
   b knows what she should do.
   c doesn't know what to do.

3 Jenny
   a agrees with Dave.
   b doesn't agree with Dave.
   c thinks Dave is right.

4 Jenny thinks
   a Tanya should send Danny an email.
   b Tanya should phone Danny.
   c Tanya should forget Danny.

5 Martha
   a thinks Tanya should contact Danny.
   b doesn't think Tanya should forget Danny.
   c doesn't think Tanya should contact Danny.

5 Extension *Listen to me!*

Give advice to these people.

I think you should ...   I don't think you should ...

Adults ....

The leader of your country ....

Your favourite pop star ....

Yourself ....

1 Dialogue completion

Matt's planning to visit the USA. He's talking to his American friend Lee.
Complete the conversation. Choose the right questions from the list (a–h).

MATT: ¹ _d_

LEE: Yes, you should. New York's a fantastic city.

MATT: ² ....

LEE: You should go to Washington too.

MATT: ³ ....

LEE: By Greyhound Bus. You can get a cheap student ticket.

MATT: ⁴ ....

LEE: In Youth Hostels. They're cheap and you'll meet lots of other young people there.

MATT: ⁵ ....

LEE: Yes, you will. It can be cold in March.

MATT: I'd like to see a baseball match. ⁶ ....

LEE: The New York Yankees, of course – if you can get a ticket!

a	Where should I stay?
b	What's the best way to travel?
c	When should I go?
d	~~Should I go to New York?~~
e	Which team should I see?
f	What other places should I visit?
g	You should go in July.
h	Will I need warm clothes?

2 *should*: questions and short answers 13b

Put the words in the right order and make questions. Then look at the advertisements and complete the answers.

PLYMOUTH LONDON
Train £70 Plane £140
Go by City Express Coach.
ONLY £35!

SEGLA ★
The greatest name in DVDs!
See the new X300
Perhaps the best DVD on the market!

CARL FINCH
If you see this man,
call the police on
0800 969 788564

1 Tom wants a cheap ticket to London.

TOM: go / train / I / should / by ? _Should I go by train?_

ALICE: .... , you shouldn't. You should go by ....

2 Jenny wants a really good DVD player.

JENNY: get / Segla / should / a / I ? ....

NICK: .... , ...

JENNY: the X250 / get / should / I ? ....

NICK: .... , ... You ....

3 Andy thinks he can see Carl Finch in the street.

ANDY: do / should / what / we ? ....

JAMES: I think we ....

3 Extension *Which train should he catch?*

Joe lives in Exeter. He wants to meet a friend in Totnes at quarter to ten. He mustn't be late.
He can't get to Exeter station before quarter to eight. Which train should he catch?

Train	Exeter	Newton Abbot	Totnes	Plymouth
A	7.37	——	8.17	8.41
B	8.05	8.28	——	9.03
C	8.25	——	9.04	9.29
D	9.12	9.37	9.52	10.13

He ....
....

Unit 11 Learning diary

Date _____

At the end of Unit 11, I can:

	Easy	Not bad	Difficult

● say what is and isn't possible, using *can* and *can't*.   ☐ ☐ ☐

At the sports centre you can _____ .

Wayne _____ walk because his leg is broken.

● talk about rules and things that are necessary or important, using *must* and *mustn't*.   ☐ ☐ ☐

We're late. We _____ be quick.

You _____ swim here. It's very dangerous.

● give my opinion and give advice, using *should* and *shouldn't*.   ☐ ☐ ☐

I think people _____ be honest.

Parents should _____ .

Ben is always late. He _____ go to bed so late.

You should go. = _____ (*in my language*)

You must go. = _____

● ask and answer questions with *should*.   ☐ ☐ ☐

What _____ I do?   You _____ telephone the police.

_____ we invite Lisa?   Yes, we _____ .   No, we _____ .

KEY WORDS

Verbs of action

walk _____   _____

_____   _____

_____   _____

_____   _____

Games

table tennis _____   _____

_____   _____

_____   _____

_____   _____

Unit 11 was

interesting ☐   quite interesting ☐   not very interesting ☐

12 Who cares?

1 Word work *The environment*

Put the letters in the right order and write the words.

1 There are lots of different SPALTN in our garden.   *plants*

2 Our vegetables aren't very good because the LISO isn't very rich.

3 I gave my mother some SLOWFER for her birthday.

4 We must protect the MINTEVORNEN.

5 The MITCALE is changing. Summers are much hotter now.

6 The RIA in our cities is often polluted.

7 The biggest ACONE in the world is the Pacific.

2 Key vocabulary *Everyday materials*

Complete the sentences with the words in the box.

> carton   can   battery   newspaper   cardboard box   ~~rubbish~~   packet   paint   plastic bags

1 You put   *rubbish*   in the dustbin.

2 Supermarkets give you .... for your shopping.

3 Would you like a .... of crisps?

4 You can buy milk in a bottle or a ....

5 Get a .... of lemonade. It isn't as heavy as a bottle.

6 The *Daily Mail* is an English ....

7 My watch stopped yesterday. It needs a new ....

8 A: What's in this big .... ?
   B: It's my new computer.

9 A: You've got white .... all over your clothes.
   B: I know. I'm painting my bedroom.

3 Would you like ...? Would you like to ...? G▶ 14b

What are the people saying? For each picture, write a question with *Would you like* + noun or *Would you like to* + verb.

1 ....

2 ....

3 ....

4 ....

4 Reading *Save it! Don't waste it!*

Read the text. Then read the sentences and write *T* (true), *F* (false), or *?* (the answer isn't in the text).

How much **water** do people use?

The average person in the USA uses 425 litres a day, the average Canadian 400 litres and the average European 200 litres. But a lot of people in other parts of the world use under 60 litres a day.

Did you know that every time we use the washing machine, we use 100 litres of water? Every time we have a bath, we use 80 litres. We use 10 litres every time we go to the toilet, and sometimes 4 litres when we clean our teeth.

Nearly 75% of the human body is water. Humans can't live for more than four days without it. But there are 400 million people in the world today who haven't got enough water, and the situation is getting worse. 14% of the world's surface is desert, and the deserts are getting bigger. Pollution is another problem. Every year a million children die because they drink polluted water.

Clean water is perhaps the most important thing on Earth. We mustn't waste it.

Think **water!**

1   A European uses more water than people in the USA.   ..F..

2   When you have a shower, you use about 30 litres of water.   ....

3   About a quarter of the human body is water.   ....

4   Humans can live for a long time without water.   ....

5   At the moment 400 million people haven't got enough water and the number is getting bigger.   ....

6   Sea water covers 70% of the Earth.   ....

7   The world's deserts aren't getting smaller.   ....

8   Polluted water isn't dangerous.   ....

9   Children shouldn't drink polluted water.   ....

5 Extension *My dustbin*

What's in your dustbin at home at the end of the week? How many things can you think of?

milk cartons

1 Word work *What's happening?*

Complete the sentences. Use the present continuous form of the verbs in the box.

rise   not win   destroy   ~~melt~~   disappear   die

1 The ice ___is melting___ .

2 The price of apples _____ .

3 He isn't happy because he _____

_____ .

4 The fire _____ the forest.

5 The flowers _____ .

6 The sun _____ behind
the mountains.

2 First conditional 9a

Complete the sentences. Use the verbs in the present simple or with *'ll/will* or *won't*.

1 If you ___sit___ in front of the television every evening, you ___'ll get___ bored. (*sit / get*)

2 If people only _____ fast food, they _____ healthy. (*eat / not be*)

3 If you _____ any breakfast, you _____ hungry before lunch. (*not have / be*)

4 If you _____ your brain, it _____ lazy. (*not use / get*)

5 If Lisa _____ her homework soon, she _____ it tonight. (*not start / not finish*)

6 If Jack _____ by train, he _____ in London in three hours. (*go / be*)

7 If you _____ an umbrella, you _____ wet. (*not take / get*)

8 If we _____ the environment, we _____ a home. (*destroy / not have*)

3 Consequences: *What will happen if ...?* (G) 9a

Make a sentence in the first conditional for each situation. Use the verbs in the box.

| not eat   hear   get cold   ~~not pass~~   break |

1 Jack's exams are next week, but he doesn't want to do any work.

   If he doesn't do any work, he won't pass his exams.

2 It's snowing outside, but Milly doesn't want to wear a coat.

   ....

3 John's going to sit down, but his glasses are on the chair.

   ....

4 Luke's in a café and he wants to have a beefburger, but his dinner's ready at home.

   ....

5 Gemma wants to play some loud music on her stereo, but she's waiting for a phone call from a friend.

   ....

4 Listening   The *If* poem

Listen and complete the poem.

The *If* poem

If you lose your ¹................... and socks, you'll have nothing on your ²................... .

If it never ³................... again, what ⁴................... you have to eat?

If the sun ⁵................... shine, your body will be cold.

If you live for a ⁶................... , you'll feel very ⁷................... .

But if you sing a ⁸................... song, you won't feel ⁹................... .

If you ¹⁰................... in the street, your life won't be too ¹¹................... .

And if you walk into the ¹²................... with a smile on your ¹³................... ,

You'll probably find a ¹⁴................... in the most unusual place.

5 Extension   *The Maldives*

Make six sentences about the Maldives.

1 The Maldives
2 The capital
3 270,000 people
4 The weather is
5 The temperature stays
6 It's usually sunny, but

| is Malé.   are a group of islands |
| always warm.   it rains a lot |
| live on the islands.   at about 33°C. |
| in the middle of the Indian Ocean. |
| in May and October. |

....

....

....

1 Word work *The big crossword*

Complete the crossword.

Across

1   Once, ... , three times, four times. (5)
4   Very small green vegetables. (4)
6   If you go to bed too late, you'll be .... in the morning. (5)
7   The .... in big cities is often polluted. (3)
8   A: What do you think of my T-shirt?
    B: I like .... (2)
9   If you .... a glass bottle, it'll probably break. (4)
10 Every country has got this national symbol. (4)
11 You study these when you study astronomy. (5)
15 This country sent the first man to the moon. (3)
17 Your hand is at the end of this. (3)
18 You sometimes wear this round the top of your trousers. (4)
19 If you fail this, you won't be very happy. (4)

Down

2   She brings your food at the restaurant. (8)
3   The opposite of *expensive*. (5)
4   When you're waiting for a train, you stand on the .... (8)
5   If you go .... for your holiday, it means you go to a foreign country. (6)
12 *General Sherman* is the name of a very .... tree. (4)
13 If you're good at drawing and painting, you'll enjoy this subject at school. (3)
14 The sea in the Maldives isn't hot and it isn't cold. So what's it like? (4)
15 A strange object in the sky. (It means 'unidentified flying object'.) (3)
16 The first three letters of the alphabet. (3)

2 Extension *What's your opinion?*

1   What was your favourite photo in the book? _____

    Can you say why? _____

2   Which was your favourite unit in the book? _____

    Can you say why? _____

3   Who was your favourite person in the book? _____

    Can you say why? _____

4   What was Book 2 like? Think of one word. _____

Unit 12 Learning diary

Date _____

At the end of Unit 12, I can:

	Easy	Not bad	Difficult
talk about the environment.	☐	☐	☐

We mustn't _____ water.

We should _____ newspapers and magazines.

_____ .

- ask people what they would like to do. ☐ ☐ ☐

Would you like to visit India?   Yes, I _____ .   No, I _____ .

_____ you like to dance?   Yes, please.   No, thank you.

Would you like to dance? = _____ *(in my language)*

- talk about results and consequences. ☐ ☐ ☐

If you don't do your homework, your teacher _____ angry.

If we _____ the train at 7.30, we'll arrive at 9.45.

If you _____ a map of Scotland, you _____ Ben Nevis.

KEY WORDS

The environment		Everyday materials	
rocks	_____	plastic bags	_____
soil	_____	_____	_____
_____	_____	_____	_____
_____	_____	_____	_____

Unit 12 was

interesting ☐   quite interesting ☐   not very interesting ☐

Grammar notes

Present simple

1a

AFFIRMATIVE AND NEGATIVE	
I/We/You/They	like cheese. don't like cheese.
He/She/It	likes cheese. doesn't like cheese.

In the third person singular (*he/she/it*), we normally add *s* (*he likes*). But:

- if a verb ends in *ch, sh, ss* or *o*, we add *es*.
  watch – he watches   finish – it finishes
  guess – he guesses   go – she goes

- if a verb ends in a consonant (*b, c, d, f, g,* etc.) + *y*, we change the *y* to *ies*.
  study – he studies   carry – she carries

1b

QUESTIONS AND SHORT ANSWERS
Do you/they like cheese? Yes, I do. No, they don't.
Does he/she/it like cheese? Yes, he does. No, she doesn't. (etc.)

- ***Does*** *your sister* ***go*** *to your school?*
- *What time* ***do*** *the shops* ***open***?

1c We use the present simple to talk about habits, regular activities and things that are generally true.

- *Helen always* ***wears*** *jeans.*
- *I* ***go*** *to the cinema every Saturday.*
- *Nick* ***doesn't play*** *tennis.*
- *Vegetarians* ***don't eat*** *meat.*

1d *Do/don't/does/doesn't* are parts of the present simple. But remember that *do* is also an ordinary verb.

- *Liam* ***does*** *the housework every Saturday.*
- *Do you* ***do*** *history at school?*

Past simple: regular verbs

2a

AFFIRMATIVE AND NEGATIVE	
I/He/She/It/We/You/They	finished. didn't finish.

We use the same form for all persons (*I, you, he*, etc.).

To form the past simple of regular verbs, we normally add *ed* to the infinitive (*finished, watched*). But:

- with verbs ending in *e*, we add *d*.
  live – lived   arrive – arrived

- with short verbs ending in 1 vowel + 1 consonant, we double the final consonant and add *ed*. We do the same with all verbs ending in vowel + *l*.
  stop – stopped   travel – travelled

- with verbs ending in a consonant (*b, c, d, f, g,* etc.) + *y*, we change the *y* to *ied*.
  try – tried   study – studied

2b

QUESTIONS AND SHORT ANSWERS
Did I/he/she/it/we/you/they finish? Yes, I did. No, we didn't. (etc.)

- ***Did*** *Kelly* ***pass*** *her exams?*
- *What time* ***did*** *the party* ***finish***?

2c We use the past simple to talk about past actions or situations.

- A: ***Did*** *you* ***watch*** *the match last night?*
  B: *No, I* ***didn't***.
- *When I was young I* ***didn't live*** *in England. I* ***lived*** *in Australia.*

Past simple: irregular verbs

3a Irregular verbs don't have the usual *ed* ending in the past simple.

go – **went**   buy – **bought**   see – **saw**

But, like regular verbs, they have the same form (*went*, *bought*, etc.) for all persons (*I, you, he*, etc.).

Irregular verbs list: Student's Book, page 143.

3b Like regular verbs, these verbs use *did* in questions and *didn't* in the negative form.

- A: *I **didn't go** to the sports centre yesterday.*
- B: *Where **did** you **go**?*

Past simple: *be*

4a

AFFIRMATIVE AND NEGATIVE	
I/He/She/It	was ill. wasn't ill.
We/You/They	were ill. weren't ill.

4b

QUESTIONS AND SHORT ANSWERS	
Was I good?	Yes, you were. No, you weren't.
Were you good?	Yes, I was. No, I wasn't.
Was he/she/it good?	Yes, he was. No, she wasn't. (etc.)
Were we/you/they good?	Yes, you were. No, we weren't. (etc.)

- *__Was__ your train late this morning?*
- *What __were__ your exams like?*

Present continuous

5a

AFFIRMATIVE AND NEGATIVE	
I'm He's/She's/It's We're/You're/They're	starting.
I'm not He/She/It isn't We/You/They aren't	starting.

5b

QUESTIONS AND SHORT ANSWERS	
Am I starting?	Yes, you are. No, you aren't.
Are you starting?	Yes, I am. No, I'm not.
Is he/she/it starting?	Yes, he is. No, she isn't. (etc.)
Are we/you/they starting?	Yes, you are. No, they aren't. (etc.)

- *__Are__ your friends __learning__ English?*
- *What's that man __doing__?*

5c We use the present continuous to talk about actions that are in progress now.

- *I can't come with you now. I'__m having__ lunch.*
- *Listen! Someone'__s playing__ the piano.*

5d We also use the present continuous to talk about arrangements for the future.

- A: *What __are you doing__ next Saturday?*
- B: *I'__m staying__ at home. My cousins __are coming__.*

Past continuous

6a

AFFIRMATIVE AND NEGATIVE	
I/He/She/It	was working. wasn't working.
We/You/They	were working. weren't working.

6b

QUESTIONS AND SHORT ANSWERS	
Was I working?	Yes, you were. No, you weren't.
Were you working?	Yes, I was. No, I wasn't.
Was he/she/it working?	Yes, he was. No, she wasn't. (etc.)
Were we/you/they working?	Yes, you were. No, they weren't. (etc.)

- *__Was__ Gemma __sitting__ next to Tom on the bus?*
- *Why __were__ all the people __laughing__?*

6c We use the past continuous to talk about actions that were in progress in the past.

- *I saw Tom and Gemma at the cinema. They **weren't watching** the film. They **were talking**.*

6d We can use the past continuous and the past simple in the same sentence. One action interrupts another.

| PAST SIMPLE   PAST CONTINUOUS |
- *When you **phoned** me, I **was having** a shower.*

The future: *will/won't*

7a

AFFIRMATIVE AND NEGATIVE	
I/He/She/It/We/You/They	will ('ll) win. won't win.

We use the same form for all persons (*I, you, he,* etc.). It is followed by the infinitive without *to*.

7b

QUESTIONS AND SHORT ANSWERS
Will I/he/she/it/we/you/they win? Yes, I will. No, they won't. (etc.)

- ***Will** the exams **be** easy?*
- *What time **will** the film **finish**?*

7c We use *will/won't* when we talk about future events and when we make predictions for the future.

- *I think Arsenal **will win** the European Cup this year.*
- A: *I've got this yellow top for Kate. **Will** she **like** it?*
  B: *No, she **won't wear** it. She hates yellow.*

The future: *going to*

8 We use *am/is/are + going to +* infinitive to talk about plans for the future.

- A: ***Are** you **going to have** a pizza?*
  B: *Yes, I am.*
- A: *Where **are** you **going to put** your poster?*
  B: *I**'m going to put** it above my bed.*
- A: ***Is** Fiona **going to learn** to drive?*
  B: *No, she isn't. The lessons are too expensive.*
- *I**'m not going to buy** a new mobile.*

First conditional

9a We use *If +* present simple + *will/won't* to talk about a possible future action or situation.

- *If you **eat** all that ice cream, you**'ll be** ill. (NOT If you will eat)*
- *If you get angry, people **won't listen** to you.*
- *If it **doesn't rain** tomorrow, I**'ll go** to the beach.*

9b Note the question *What will happen if ... (+ present simple)?*

- *What will happen if the ice cap **melts**?*
- *What will happen if I **fail** the exam?*

have got and *have*

10a We use *have got* to talk about:

- possessions.   *I**'ve got** some new trainers.*
- appearance.   *Fiona **has got** long hair.*
- relationships.   *I **haven't got** any uncles.*
- illnesses.   *They**'ve** both **got** a stomach ache.*

10b We use *have* to talk about activities and things we eat.

- A: *Where's Sarah?*
  B: *She's **having** a bath.*
- *We**'ll have** a great time at the party tonight.*
- *Harry always **has** cereal for breakfast.*
- *I never **have** lunch in the school canteen.*

10c The past simple of *have got* and *have* is *had / didn't have.*

- *When I was young I **had** long, fair hair.*
- *Jack couldn't go. He **didn't have** any money.*
- *What **did** you **have** for breakfast?*

can/can't

11a We use *can/can't* to talk about

- possibility.   *Rick **can go** to the match, but we **can't go**. We haven't got tickets.*
- permission.   A: ***Can I use** your mobile?*
                 B: *No, you **can't**. Sorry!*
- ability.   *I **can play** the piano a bit, but I **can't read** music.*

We use the same form for all persons (*I, you, he,* etc.). It is followed by the infinitive without *to*.

11b We often use *can/can't* with *see* and *hear*.

- *I **can see** Kate. She's in the garden.*
  (NOT ~~I see~~ Kate.)
- *I **can't hear** you. The music's too loud.*
  (NOT ~~I don't hear~~ you.)

11c *Could* and *couldn't* are the past simple forms of *can* and *can't*.

- *I **could play** the piano when I was four.*
- *Pete **couldn't go** to school yesterday.*

must/mustn't

12 We use *must/mustn't* to talk about obligation.

- A: *There's a big hole in your trousers.*
  B: *Oh, no! I **must change** them.*
- *Hurry up! We **mustn't be** late.*

should/shouldn't

13a

AFFIRMATIVE AND NEGATIVE	
I/He/She/It/We/You/They	should try. shouldn't try.

We use the same form for all persons (*I, you, he,* etc.). *Should* and *shouldn't* are followed by the infinitive without *to*.

13b

QUESTIONS AND SHORT ANSWERS
Should I/you/he/she/it/we/you/they try? Yes, I should. No, they shouldn't. (etc.)

13c We use *should/shouldn't* when we give or ask for advice and when we think something is/isn't the right thing to do.

- *You **shouldn't go** to London by train. You **should go** by coach. It's cheaper.*
- *We **shouldn't waste** water.*
- *There's a snake in the kitchen. What **should** I **do**?*

like/love/enjoy/hate

14a When a verb follows *like, love, enjoy* or *hate*, we normally use the *-ing* form.

- A: *What do you like **doing**?*
  B: *I enjoy **swimming**. I don't like **doing** the housework. I hate **getting** up early.*

14b When a verb follows *would like*, we use the infinitive with *to*.

- *Would you like **to go** to the cinema?*
  (NOT *Would you like ~~going~~?*)
- *I'd like **to visit** Africa one day.*
  (NOT *I'd like ~~visiting~~.*)

Polite offers and requests

15a We use *Would you like* and *Could I* in polite offers and requests.

- ***Would you like** to come to my party?*
- ***Could I** stay at your house tomorrow night?*

15b We normally use *some* (NOT *any*) in polite offers and requests.

- ***Would you like** an egg or **some** cereal?*
- ***Could I** have **some** cheese and an apple?*

Short forms

16a Note the short forms.

I am	I'm	is not	isn't
He is	He's	are not	aren't
It is	It's	was not	wasn't
Helen is	Helen's	were not	weren't
We are	We're		
They are	They're	does not	doesn't
		do not	don't
I have got	I've got	did not	didn't
It has got	It's got		
Jack has got	Jack's got	has not	hasn't
You have got	You've got	have not	haven't
I will	I'll	will not	won't
She will	She'll	would not	wouldn't
You will	You'll	cannot	can't
		could not	couldn't
I would	I'd	should not	shouldn't
They would	They'd	must not	mustn't

We use short forms when we speak and when we write emails or letters to friends. We use full forms when we write more formal texts.

16b Note these alternative forms:

– For *he/she/it isn't*, we can also say *he's not*, etc.

– For *we/you/they aren't*, we can say *we're not*, etc.

there is / there are

17a We use *there is* (*there's*) + singular noun and *there are* + plural noun to say that something exists.

- **There's** a sports shop in King Street.
- **There are** 31 students in my class.
- A: **Is there** a swimming pool at your school?
  B: No, **there isn't**.

17b We use *there is* (NOT *there are*) in a list if the first thing is singular.

- Our flat is quite small. **There's** a kitchen, a living room and two bedrooms.

17c We use *there was/wasn't/were/weren't* for the past.

- **There was** a great film on TV last night.
- **There weren't** any cars in the 17th century.
- A: **Were there** many people at the concert?
  B: Yes, **there were**.

17d We use *there is/are* when we talk about something for the first time. Then we use *it is / they are* to give more information.

- **There's** a spider in your hair. **It's** quite big.
- **There are** two churches here. **They're** very old.

Countable and uncountable nouns

18a Countable nouns are things that we can count. They've got a plural form.

a dog – two dogs   a boat – some boats

18b Uncountable nouns are things that we can't count (*music, water, bread, information*, etc.). We use *some/any* with these nouns (NOT *a/an*), and they haven't got a plural form.

- I'd like **some advice**. (NOT ~~an advice~~ or ~~advices~~.)
- Have we got **any milk**? (NOT ~~a milk~~ or ~~milks~~)

18c Some nouns can be countable or uncountable (*lemonade, coffee, cheese, chicken*, etc.).

Countable: I'd like two **lemonades**, please.
                (= two cans/glasses of lemonade)
Uncountable: I'll buy **some lemonade** for the party.

some and any

19a We use *some* and *any* to talk about an indefinite quantity or number. We normally use *some* in affirmative sentences, and *any* in negative sentences and questions (but see 19b).

We use *some* and *any* before plural nouns.

- A: If you're hungry, there are **some** beefburgers, but we haven't got **any** onions.
  B: Have we got **any** tomatoes?
  A: Yes, there are **some** in the fridge.
  (We can use *some/any* on their own, without a noun.)

We also use them before uncountable nouns.

- I want **some** paint. Have we got **any** white paint?

19b We use *some* in questions to make an offer or a request. (See also 15b.)

- Would you like **some** cheese?
- Can I have **some** milk, please?

19c We don't use *some* when we talk about things or people in general.

- I'd like some pasta, please.
  BUT: I like pasta.
- We saw some dolphins yesterday.
  BUT: I love dolphins.

a lot of / lots of, much and many

20a We use *a lot of* or *lots of* with countable and uncountable nouns to describe a large number or quantity. We normally use them in affirmative sentences.

- There were **a lot of / lots of** people at the party.
- English people eat **a lot of / lots of** Italian food.

But we can use them in questions and negative sentences too.

- Are there **lots of** tourists here?
- I haven't got **a lot of** time.

20b We use *much* with uncountable nouns to describe a quantity of something. We normally use it in questions and negative sentences.

- How **much** money have you got?
- Hurry up! We haven't got **much** time.

20c We use *many* with plural nouns to describe a number of people or things. We normally use it in questions and negative sentences.

- *How **many** English friends have you got?*
- *There aren't **many** cinemas in our town.*

But we sometimes use it at the beginning of affirmative sentences.

- ***Many** English people go on holiday to Spain.*

Position of adjectives

21a Adjectives go before the noun in English. The form always stays the same.

- *I've got some **fantastic** computer games.*
- *'Alien' was a very **scary** film.*
- *She's a really **optimistic** person.*

21b Note the position of these adjectives in expressions of measurement.

- *This tree is about 10 metres **tall**.*
- *The cathedral's 500 years **old**.*
- *Mount Kilimanjaro is 5,895 metres **high**.*
- *The swimming pool's 2 metres **deep**.*
- *My room is 3.5 metres **long** and 3 metres **wide**.*

Comparatives and superlatives

22a With short adjectives (*tall, nice, old*, etc.) we add *er* or *r* to form the comparative, and *est* or *st* to form the superlative.

Comparative:

- *A giraffe's tall**er** than an elephant.*
- A: *Is your brother old**er** than you?*
  B: *No, he's young**er**. And he's nic**er** than me.*

Superlative:

*What's the tall**est** building in the world?*

22b With most adjectives of two syllables (*fa-mous*) we use *more* and *the most* to form the comparative and the superlative.

- *I want to be **more famous** than Picasso.*
- *I think history is **the most boring** subject.*

But with adjectives ending in consonant + *y* (*easy, happy*, etc.) we use *ier/iest*.

- *English is **easier** than Chinese, but it isn't **the easiest** language.*

22c With long adjectives we use *more / the most*.

- *The film was **more exciting** than the book.*
- *Your computer's faster than mine, but it was **more expensive**.*
- *Sarah always buys **the most expensive** clothes in the shop.*
- *The last question in the exam was **the most difficult**.*

22d Note these irregular comparative and superlative forms.

good   –   better   the best
bad   –   worse   the worst

as ... as ...

23 We use *as ... as ...* to say that two things or people are the same, and *not as ... as ...* to say they're different.

- *My brother's only seven, but he's **as tall as** me.*
- *A Saab isn't **as expensive as** a Porsche, but it isn't **as fast**.*
- *Is Amy **as good as** Zoe at tennis?*

Expressions of frequency

24 Note the use of *a* in these time expressions.

- *I have a guitar lesson **twice a week**.*
- *We visit my grandparents **three times a year**.*
- *Take this medicine **once a day**.*

Frequency adverbs

25a We use frequency adverbs to say how often something happens.

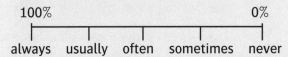

100%   0%

always   usually   often   sometimes   never

25b Frequency adverbs usually go before the main verb.

- *My mum **never** eats mushrooms.*
- *Do you **always** work in the evening?*
- *She **often** went to clubs when she was young.*

But they go after the verb *be*.

- *I was **often** ill when I was small.*
- *Dolphins aren't **usually** dangerous.*

Possessive 's

26a We use 's to show that something belongs to someone. We add 's to a singular noun.

- This is **Sadie's** watch.
- The **dog's** name is Sam.

With two nouns or names we add 's to the second.

- I stayed at my **aunt and uncle's** house.
- I'm going to **Pete and Kathy's** party.

26b We can use the possessive form without the noun.

- A: Whose is this bag?
- B: It's **Rick's**. (= Rick's bag)

26c With plural nouns ending in s, we only add an apostrophe (').

- This is my **grandparents'** house.

But with irregular plural nouns, we add 's.

- It's a **women's** magazine.

Possessive adjectives and pronouns

27a

I →	my	mine	we →	our	ours
he →	his	his	you →	your	yours
she →	her	hers	they →	their	theirs
it →	its	—			

Note that there isn't a possessive pronoun for *it*.

27b Adjectives: note the use of *his* and *her*.

- **David** and **his** wife, Victoria. (David → **his**)
- **Victoria** and **her** husband, David. (Victoria → **her**)

We use *its* when the possessor is an animal or a thing.

- The blue whale is really big. **Its** heart weighs 450 kilos!

27c Pronouns

- A: Are these shoes **yours**, Danny?
- B: No. Ask Peter. I think they're **his**.
- A: Whose is this anorak?
  (or Whose anorak is this?)
- B: It's **mine**.

Object pronouns

28a

I →	me	it →	it	you →	you
he →	him	we →	us	they →	them
she →	her				

28b We use an object pronoun when it isn't necessary to repeat a noun.

- Where are my socks? Can you see **them**?
  (them = my socks)

28c We put object pronouns after the main verb, or after a preposition.

- I love **you**. (NOT ~~I you love~~.)
- Where's Sarah? I can't see **her**.
  (NOT ~~I can't her see~~.)
- Wait **for us**! We're coming!
- Is Jack going too? I don't want to go **with him**.

28d Don't forget the object pronoun!

These are my new trousers. Do you like **them**?
(NOT ~~Do you like?~~)

- A: What do you think of my pizza?
- B: Mmm! I like **it**. (NOT ~~I like~~.)

Prepositions

29a *in/on/at* for place and time.

- She lives **in** Paris. Her family's **in** Spain.
- Jack's **in** bed. He was **in** hospital last week.
- There was a number **on** the door.
- She isn't **at** home. She's **at** the cinema.
- I was born **in** 1993.
- My birthday's **in** June. It's **on** 10th June.
- I'll see you **on** Friday.
- Do you work **in** the evening?
- My sister goes shopping **at** the weekend.
- I get up **at** 7.30.

29b We use prepositions (*across, up, past,* etc.) to show the direction of movement.

- The dog swam **across** the lake.
- I walked **up** the hill.
- I ran **down** the hill.
- She walked **along** the river.
- We went **past** Buckingham Palace.
- We ran **through** the trees to the house.